WITHDRAWN
FROM
COLLECTION

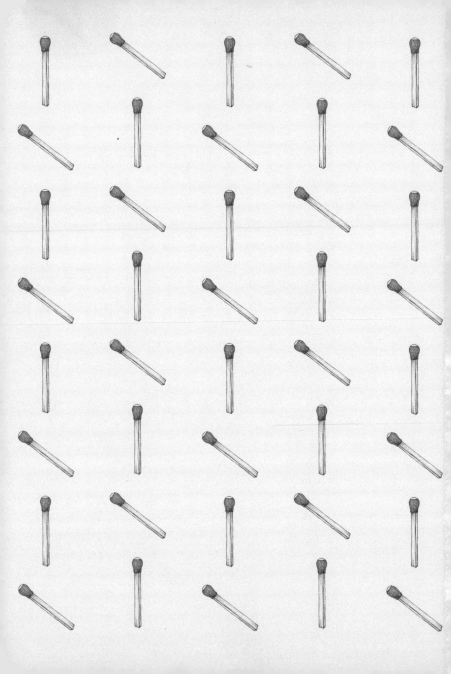

HOW TO BUILD A FIRE

HEARTH | HOME | STOVES | CABINS
CAMPGROUNDS | SURVIVAL

J. SCOTT DONAHUE

CIDER MILL PRESS

BOOK
PUBLISHERS
KENNEBUNKPORT, MAINE

13-Digit ISBN: 978-1604337006
10-Digit ISBN: 1604337001

This book may be ordered by mail
from the publisher. Please include
$5.99 for postage and handling.
Please support your local book-
seller first!

Books published by Cider Mill
Press Book Publishers are available at special discounts for bulk
purchases in the United States by
corporations, institutions, and
other organizations. For more
information, please contact the
publisher.

Cider Mill Press Book Publishers
"Where good books are ready
for press"
PO Box 454
12 Spring Street
Kennebunkport, Maine 04046
Visit us on the Web!
www.cidermillpress.com

Cover and interior design
by Debbie Berne
Illustrations by Gina Baek
Other art and images used under
official license from Shutterstock

Printed in China
1 2 3 4 5 6 7 8 9 0

First Edition

CONTENTS

FIRE IS NEVER A GENTLE MASTER.

−PROVERB

INTRODUCTION

We told our first stories sitting around a fire. Poets recited epics centering around super-human athletes, cunning thieves, or tricksters shaped like the animals familiar to the land. All of these mythical characters somehow bestowed upon humankind a strange, wondrous light. The very moment we held this light, we instantly separated ourselves from the animal world. We held a light that warmed our bare skin in the winter, cooked our food, warded off predators, and captured our imaginations. Our mastery of this light proved our control over nature—or at least gave us the illusion of it.

So precious was fire, as these poets told their rapt audience, that it had to be stolen from on high. There was Prometheus—the original runner of the Olympic torch—who stole fire from Mount Olympus to give the Greeks. There was Grandmother Spider, who smuggled embers in a clay pot to give to the Cherokee. There was Azazel and a cohort of miscreant angels who taught the ancient Hebrews to how to make fire, deliberately stepping on the toes of a jealous god. There was also Matarisvan from the *Rigveda*, and Nanobozho of Ojibwe people, and endless other heroes and anti-heroes. Sitting near a fire and listening to these stories, we must've felt great kinship with these brazen fire thieves. How difficult it is to understand how–in only one hundred years–we've all but forgotten the very basics of making fire from simple means. To reconnect with the ones who gave us fire, we must go back 1.5 to 2 million years and learn from our descendants.

To pinpoint a precise moment when our ancestors discovered fire is impossible. Anthropologists struggle with the question of fire's role as a catalyst to human evolution. Our use of fire, however, indisputably influenced the evolution of human culture. Charles Darwin once famously stated that the discovery of fire was "probably the greatest ever made by man, excepting language." Again, we told our first stories sitting around a fire.

"Before enlightenment, chopping wood and carrying water. After enlightenment, chopping wood and carrying water." —**HSIN HSIN MING**

We–and when I say "we," I mean those ancestors of the *Homo* genus with whom we share a common ancestry, and the ones who passed their ingenious, fire-carrying genes down to us–discovered fire long before we needed it. As *Homo erectus*, we carried the first fire nearly two million years ago. Maybe one of us found hot coals smoldering in a lightning-killed tree, or at the foot of a volcano, or at the rim of a charred meadow. Something about the glowing red caught our eyes and spurred our curious and opportunistic brains. We would carry these smoldering embers back to our encampments in clay, hollow logs, or in cradles of moss and bone. Between 1.8 and 1.9 million years ago, our *H. erectus* bodies had already acquired new, advantageous, and adaptive traits as our dependence on fire grew. Our brains had grown to an average 1000 cm^3, double the size of the more ape-like *H. habilis*. We hunted by stalking and running our prey to death. Our bare skin became advantageous over body hair. (*The Naked Ape* famously posits that perhaps we looked sexier without all that hair everywhere.) Our digestive systems and pallets yearned for the flavor of cooked meat with its fat dripping from the stick and roots softened and made edible by boiled water (boiled water meant safe drinking too).

Supplemental use of fire eventually became necessity. The earliest evidence of the first, habitually used fires can be found across the world's caves in Africa, Europe, and the Middle East, scattered across the world like telltale shards of burnt bone. The oldest campfire site dates back to at least one million years ago, found in South Africa's Wonderwerk cave. Excavators found cooked animal remains. They also found chips of flint, which point to another question: Were our ancestors making arrowheads, or they were trying to create sparks by striking stones?

Clearly, "stealing" fire—or in our case, foraging for it from nature—could not sustain the progress of our species. So we invented fire.

We may have made our first fires with wood-on-wood friction. Nearing the end of the Lower Paleolithic era some 500,000 years ago, we began to make fire with tools made of wood, string, and stone. With teardrop-shaped hand axes of flint, chert, and agate, we hacked through bone, scraped skin off of meat, made sharper weapons, and chopped wood. It's hard to say when we started making fire with only wood.

Building the first form of "friction fire" required the kind of ingenuity only humans have. As we began to build fires, we began thinking about "if-then" outcomes. If we rub hard wood against soft wood, then wood shavings form; if we continue rubbing, then smoke appears; if smoke appears, then coals will form; if wind is too strong, then coals will go out; if there is a slight breeze, then coals will grow; and so on, went our scientific minds.

Over time, we developed and improved upon our crude ways to make fire. There was the fire plough (pg. 106) that required a great deal of craftsmanship, not to mention patience and practice—and especially tough hands. The hand drill technique (pg. 102) similarly required a keen understanding of friction embers. We figured out that a slight breeze can keep a glowing coal going, and recognized patterns in the smoldering dust we made: *black, smoking dust makes fire.*

Here's an aside: For anyone who has tried drilling for fire, show me the blisters on your palms to prove it. The spindle method is time-consuming, laborious, painful, and seemingly impossible. Only experienced survivalists have perfected this means to make fire—a skill that does wonders for YouTube channel hits. Undoubtedly, an existence spent drilling and plowing wood against wood inspired in us to invent more efficient, less infuriating ways to make fire from scratch. So we modified the drill with ropes. We added stone weights. We incorporated bows to do the work for us. This was all Stone Age machinery—the bow drill (pg. 109) and pump drill (pg. 113) methods—invented to save our poor skin.

"Fire is the most tolerable third party."
—**HENRY DAVID THOREAU**

Once we had a good fire going, we sent a message to the snarling predators that lurked beyond our encampments: a message of dominance. Fire could keep wolves at bay, except for the curious ones. Fire attracted wolves to our side. And who could blame them? The irresistible scent of roasted meat, discarded bones and scraps, the rewarding sensation of a scratch behind the ear, and especially the belly rub came in exchange for loyalty. Wolves that depended on us became our protectors, and we bred those protectors for thousands of years. Fire gave us our proverbial best friends in dogs.

At the dawn of the Bronze Age, stone lost its luster. People 5,000 years ago figured out a way to use fire to mine for copper and bronze. Called "fire-setting," the trick involved placing fire near a rock face, and then dousing the rock with cold water to fracture open the rock to reveal the dazzling metals within. These metals, with the help of fire, could be melted, pounded into shape, sharpened more easily, and traded at a more valuable price than stone. Then bronze and copper tools gave way to iron.

Iron—namely steel, which we manipulated to our design with our mastery of fire—put civilization on a fast track. Steel meant superior knives and axes, more hygienic cookware and utensils, and trusty hammers and nails to build cities that stood plumb and proud for centuries. However, the fundamental advancement of iron was using it to make fire. Rather than chipping crudely away at stones with marcasite or pyrite, we forged and shaped iron to make artificial flints. These looked like bracelets: oblong-shaped, with a side for gripping and another side with a course surface that gave off sparks with the brush of a blade. And unlike stone, these could last thousands of strikes without losing their integrity. Iron strikers were such a marvelous invention that we used them until matches could be mass-produced in the mid-nineteenth century.

At some point in our innovative partnership with fire, we learned ways of powering our lives far beyond the kitchen and hearth. During the Industrial Revolution, we burned coal to power factories, locomotives, and steam ships.

Around fire we developed culture. Religious rites, dances, sacrifices, and funerals all involved fire, with its creative and destructive power. In fire we found creative answers to explain the mysteries of life. Zoroastrianism, one of the world's oldest religions, treats fire as a purifying medium through which celestial judgment is passed. The Hindu deity, Agni, is the avatar of fire and sacrifice, and appears in the flames accepting sacrifices from the faithful. And in Exodus, the god of Abraham communicates with Moses in the form of a burning bush. Fire was and continues to be a meeting point between god(s) and us.

Prometheus saw the way mankind starved, shivered in caves, and succumbed to wild beasts. His pity for primitive man spurred him to charity. If we humans simply had fire, we could be better off than the beasts that hunted us. Over five thousand of years after this Greek myth was

DON'T TOUCH!

What kind of instincts do we have that help us build fire? One study, conducted in 2012 by UCLA evolutionary anthropologist Daniel Fessler, suggests that most adults in the West are fascinated with fire as a result of not having mastered the art of building fire as a child. Perhaps the reason you're reading this book now is because you didn't learn as a kid. Better late than never.

Imagine being a cave-child, where instead of *Sesame Street* you had paintings of saber-toothed tigers, or gazelles, or mammoths that dwarfed a group of hunters. You'd have to learn at an early age how not to be eaten; and you had to learn everything you could possibly know about how to make fire. Think of how alluring a flame is if the first instructions you are given are **Don't touch!** We hear these instructions at the same age we hear **Look both ways when crossing the street.** At this same age we obsess over predators, both real and imaginary: dinosaurs, wolves, lions, and the boogeyman under the bed. Of course children will be curious; the tips of their fingers get close to an open flame, but linger there, getting a grasp of the threshold between inexplicable warmth and a first-degree burn.

first told, we have already begun—as if the gods all along had revenge in mind for our fire-thieving ways—to see the consequences of our gluttony for burning. They manifest in polluted air, wildfires, and suffocating global temperatures. Fire—in the form of fossil fuel combustion, wildfires, and the calamities they trigger—threatens our very existence.

We never had the innate ability to create fire from scratch. Nor did we possess genetic instructions on how to chop and stack wood the right way, or even how to smother a fire, let alone how to use fire to slow-cook a wild boar. Unlike orb weavers that build Gothic webs from a blueprint in their DNA, we can only put fire to use by learning how to do it from someone else. Here's where I come in: As the strapping young author of this book, I gladly accept the responsibility of teaching you all that I have collected and learned about building a fire from our ancestors. Let's keep the fire going.

"Climb the mountains and get their good tidings. Nature's peace will flow into you as sunshine flows into trees." —**JOHN MUIR**, *OUR NATIONAL PARKS*

CHAPTER 1

THE ART OF SPLITTING WOOD

ONE TOUCH
of NATURE
MAKES
THE WHOLE
WORLD KIN.

—WILLIAM SHAKESPEARE

I SWUNG MY FIRST AXE when I was ten years old. Gripping the handle of my grandfather's axe with two hands, the tool was too much. I lifted it with chest muscles I didn't know I had. The head of the axe wobbled above my parted hair on a crisp November morning. The log I intended to split was perched on a chopping stump, waiting for me to do my worst.

I remember muttering *one, two, three*, before my arms swung down with all my might. My eyes clamped closed, and *whack* went the axe, sticking into the wood. The sound of splintering chips and a *shink* of steel surprised me. The axe handle stunned my hands the way a baseball bat did on a cold morning. When I opened my eyes, the cedar log was untouched. *Swing and a miss.*

As a ten-year-old, I had no idea just what I was doing with an axe, and upon further reflection, I was using the tool all wrong. Chopping wood is a lot like the exquisite craft of needlepoint: solitary, intricate, and even therapeutic; and best of all, you get to handle a sharp object. But like any other refined craft, proper wood chopping requires a great deal of precision and accuracy. Accurate wood chopping technique requires you to hone in on a near-perfect bisection of wood, whereas precise wood chopping depends on your consistency and repetition in this pursuit of a more perfectly parsed piece of wood. So for god's sake, keep your eyes open.

TOOLS

Axe. The first axe, dating 1.5 million years ago to the Acheulean period, was a wedge of chert shaped like a teardrop. It doesn't take a trip to the hardware store to know that a modern axe is a far cry from such an archaic specimen—and yet they share an obvious blueprint. Both modern and ancient stone axes are defined by a center of gravity concentrated behind a wedge: the butt weighing down a blade. By adding a haft to the stone (eventually bronze and iron) axe, we achieved more leverage, which meant more force for less work.

Like choosing the right baseball bat, pick the axe according to your own height and strength. For beginners,

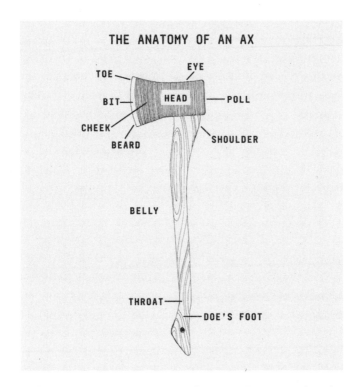

THE ANATOMY OF AN AX

TOE
EYE
BIT
HEAD
POLL
CHEEK
BEARD
SHOULDER
BELLY
THROAT
DOE'S FOOT

a five-pound axe head is sufficient. Also, consider the length of the handle. Long hafts give the user an advantage of greater force on the chop; however, shorter axes allow for more accuracy and control.

For the express purpose of splitting wood, find a single-bit axe with a concave cheek. While a splitting maul or specialized splitting axe is better suited for this purpose, a felling axe is usable for splitting wood. This particular shape ensures a quick and easy bisection of the wood, while preventing the head from sticking. Hafts are usually made of hickory or ash. Hickory is a mainstay for axes, with its compressed grain and shock resistance. Ash, similarly, is good enough for major league baseball bats. And while wood inevitably wears down, or develops chips and cracks, they're easy to replace. When it comes to handles, varnish *sucks*. A varnished handle chips more easily after use, is hard on your hands, and is more slippery than an untreated handle.

There's rustic craftsmanship and constant maintenance of a wood haft—and then there's fiberglass. These handles last forever and require no maintenance. That said, unless you're splitting and stacking six cords every winter, the added durability of fiberglass won't matter much.

A RUSTY AXE IS AN EASY FIX. Using steel wool or course grit sandpaper that contains aluminum oxide or silicon carbide, rub the axe head in a circular, buffing motion. When the rust is sufficiently removed, take a rag and metal polish for a new-blade sheen. To keep your tools from rusting again, apply linseed or even motor oil.

Splitting Maul. It's almost more like a medieval broadsword than an axe. The splitting maul weighs twice as

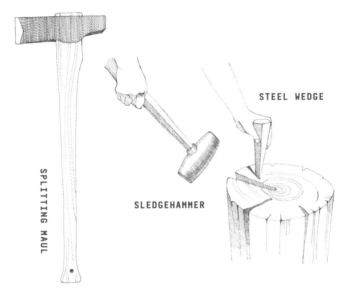

SPLITTING MAUL

STEEL WEDGE

SLEDGEHAMMER

much as a typical axe and comes equipped with a sledge-hammer on the opposite end. Mauls have the stock of a sledgehammer too, unlike the ergonomically curved handle of an axe. The blade of a maul is a broad wedge which also keeps it from sticking in the wood, as opposed to an axe's thin, fanned beard that can easily get stuck.

Steel Wedge and Sledgehammer. Think of an axe, disassembled into two functioning parts. Hammer-tap the wedge until it fits snuggly into a groove and—like a nail in the wall—let it stand, ready to be driven in. Use a heavy, mid-sized sledgehammer in the same motion as a hatchet or axe. One thing to consider when using the steel wedge: Your first whack better do the job and split all the way through. The irony of a wedge is that can get lodged to a point of no return, especially if you are cutting into a stump of hickory or birch—and then you'll have walk to your neighbor's house, shame-faced, and ask to borrow his axe.

Hatchet. Few tools inspire as much reverence and ardor for wood splitting as the hatchet. The hatchet is the

Goldilocks of hewing tools: heftier than a knife, too stunted to be an axe—and it fulfills the tasks of both tools, *just right*. A shingle hatchet can be operated with one hand, and used for chopping on one side, and hammering on the other. Required reading for any user of the hatchet is Gary Paulsen's award-winning Young Adult book of the same name.

Hatchets are more useful in cabin and campground environs than they are in the backcountry. Since they usually weigh in at two to three pounds, a hatchet would do more to weigh you down than your trusty knife. With that said, the hatchet is the finest and fastest tool to separate kindling out of larger pieces of fuelwood. Using a hatchet as opposed to the baton method guarantees less sweat, and a more finessed cut—especially with more dense wood like birch.

TO TEST YOUR BLADE'S SHARPNESS, take a slanted hack at a piece of firewood. If the blade is dull, it'll glance right off the wood. A sharp blade should catch into the side with little effort.

Folding Pocketknife. Two mantras will be refrained throughout this book for starting a great fire: *Start small*,  and *You will need a knife.* The pocketknife fulfills both. A small ember can't grow without dry, fluffy tinder to serve as a cradle. Since small jobs require small tools, use a fine blade to shave and string apart a piece of dry wood. A pocketknife, or any other type of retractable knife ranging from one to four inches, will do for shaving off splinters, strings, and chips—and other elements that are crucial for a tinder ball (pg. 70). Shave and strip the wood until you have enough to cup with both hands.

Pocketknives are also crucial for shaping wood into crude fire-starting tools if need be.

Fixed-Blade Hunting Knife. For the same reason we use a steak knife to trim tri-tip, a serrated hunting knife proves its effectiveness by carving into dense sticks and logs. You don't have to have a foot-long knife like Rambo's in *First Blood;* unless you're trying to compensate for something else, a fixed-blade hunting knife doesn't need to be more than six inches.

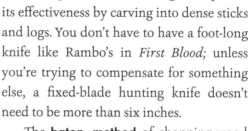

The **baton method** of chopping wood requires only a sturdy hunting knife to split through a dense piece of wood.

First, working from the outside in, you lodge the blade into the fuelwood or kindling you wish to split. This may take a few good whacks or a few taps from a blunt object to sink the knife sufficiently into the wood.

.THE BATON METHOD

It helps to knock the bottom of the kindling against a hard surface (i.e., a chopping block). The percussion against the bottom of the log will drive the blade deeper into the wood. Repeat this action until the piece is sufficiently split.

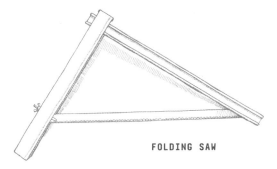

FOLDING SAW

Folding Saw. Concerning camping and backcountry trips, these bad boys are lightweight alternatives to the hatchet—stark differences in use aside. Folding saws usually have a rubber handle and require laborious back-and-forth action, rather than a satisfying, one-and-done chop of a hatchet. These are best for hewing saplings or feathery branches to make shelter, but not so much for assembling firewood.

RECOMMENDED FOR SAFETY

Gloves. Some work gloves are dipped in latex-rubber; while this aids in keeping a good grip with a saw, they aren't recommended for chopping or hammering in a wedge. For those splitting chores, you need gloves that will keep your hands from getting cold, chapped, or blistered, while allowing free movement from the axe's shoulder to its throat on the downswing.

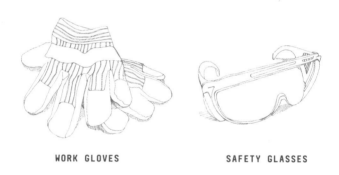

WORK GLOVES   SAFETY GLASSES

Glasses. Have you ever seen a lumberjack cry? If so, it's for no other reason than a piece of wood lodging itself in an eyelid and triggering a tear. Otherwise, a safe wood worker avoids this painful situation—often mistaken for a moment of emotional vulnerability—by wearing protective eyewear.

Heavy boots. If you need any reason to wear heavy or even steel-toed boots while standing at the chopping block, think of the baseball commentator's mantra: "Swing and a miss." Boots are simply common sense when dealing with heavy chunks of wood and a sharp object.

CHOPPING AND SPLITTING

HOW TO SAFELY SWING AN AXE

A glancing blow to the shin is an all-too-common injury. It's better to aggressively follow the rules and play it safe than end up in the hospital!

1. Clear the area around you. There shouldn't be any roots, rocks, trees, or branches within an axe-length (the length of your axe and your arm) of you and your logs.

2. Create an "axe yard" by measuring two axe-lengths around, and make a boundary to show others that there are sharp edges nearby.

3. Make a chopping block by sawing a log so that it is about two feet high, and standing it upright.

4 Make it easy on yourself and aim for cracks in the log first. Avoid knots and turn a log over so the knots are on the bottom, allowing for the bit to hit clean wood first. If you get tired, rest!

Line up your swing and make sure the area is clear around you.

Hold the shoulder with your dominant hand, and place your other hand low on the handle.

⑤ When you're not cutting wood with your axe,
muzzle it with its sheath. If one isn't around,
avoid that lumberjack temptation of throwing
it over your shoulder. Instead, point the cutting
edge down and away from you as you walk.

Your dominant hand will
slide on the downswing to
meet your bottom hand.

Swing downward
forcefully onto the
awaiting piece of wood.

DON'T FELL A TREE (UNLESS YOU MUST)

Trees are perfectly content with staying in the ground. And unless the tree is on your private property, trees should stay put. With that said, if you want to fell a tree on your own property, then you need to do it safely. Hiring properly trained professionals or using a chainsaw is a heck of a lot easier than whacking away with an axe.

In parks and campgrounds, it's surprisingly common for people to fell live trees only to discover green wood won't burn. Make it a practice to collect downed, dry wood, which *will* burn—and not anger any park rangers in the process.

Ok. If you absolutely must fell a tree to use for firewood, here's how:

❶ Do not stand in front of the tree, but rather offset yourself so the tree is in front of your lead foot (opposite of your dominant side).

❷ Starting at a 45-degree angle, chop a V-shaped notch (called a **kerf**) into the trunk of the tree from the angle in which you want it to fall. Continue chopping at the tree at a 45-degree angle until you cut into the radius of the trunk.

❸ On the opposite side of the tree, cut another notch into the tree—this time two inches above your other cut. The cut creates a hinge.

❹ Expand the width of the first kerf in an upward direction until it approaches the height of the second kerf. As the tree starts to lean and crack, take your escape route—45 degrees from the back of the feet and 15 feet away.

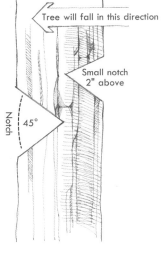

Tree will fall in this direction

Small notch 2" above

Notch 45°

❺ After you've felled the tree, you'll have to **buck** the wood into smaller pieces. Stand with the log in front of you, with your legs shoulder-width apart. Bring your axe above your shoulder and swing down between your legs, then bring your axe back up to the opposite shoulder and swing down from that side. Similarly to how you felled the tree, cut a V-shape into half of the log at a 45 degree angle, until the notches meet.

SPLIT-FIT

HOW TO GET LUMBERJACK MUSCLES

Splitting wood makes vigorous exercise out of a
chore. A couple hours of wielding an axe and hewing firewood can give you a strong heart, Popeye
forearms, and a solid core. You'll also gain a measure of endurance and hand-eye coordination in all
that mindless repetition. **Disclaimer:** The one thing
splitting wood can't do is help you grow a thick
beard, let alone fill in those missing patches on
your cheek.

The action of lifting an axe targets the upper
back, shoulder, and bicep muscles, while the downswing requires your abdominal muscles to engage
and curl. And like weight lifting, your gains
in fitness depend on the proper technique. Once
you understand the correct motion in all of its
parts, you can turn it into one fluid and effective motion.

1. Grasp the axe's shoulder with your dominant
   hand, and place your other hand low on the
   grip. The dominant hand will slide while your
   other hand will provide crucial leverage on the
   downswing. The axe blade should be facing downward and the shaft parallel to the ground.

2 Raise the axe over your head. As the axe reaches the apex directly above your head, slide your dominant hand down the shaft. The dominant hand will slide down to meet your other hand. Don't forget legwork. Your legs should go into a quarter-squat, while your feet should be a little more than shoulder-width apart and square to the wood you are cutting.

3 Swing the axe downward forcefully onto the awaiting piece of wood. For extra velocity of the tool, snap your wrists along with the axe. Your hands should create a fulcrum-lever motion that will give you that extra **thunk!**

An hour at the chopping block burns 400 to 500 calories—or more if you're doing it in the dead of winter.

SHARPENING AN AXE

No wonder we "keep our nose to the grindstone" when faced with tedious work; sharpening an axe takes repetitive strokes. There's little doubt that pedal grindstones–used as far back as 15th century–can hone an axe to perfection. But for DIY purposes, all you will need are these:

- Bastard file
- Vice
- Circular whetstone (also called a "puck")
- Linseed oil
- Leather gloves

First, stick the axe head securely in the vice with the edge pointed outward. With a file, slide lightly along the edge as if to gently blunt the blade. This action removes chips and nicks along the blade edge. Keep going until the rough edge becomes smoothed out under the file. This will create burrs–shiny flecks of exposed metal–on each side of the blade.

Next, grab the file with both hands end to end. At an angle of roughly 25 to 30 degrees, slide the file downward into the blade–and only this direction–all along the edge. The leather gloves should protect your fingers in this process. Remove the new burrs you made with the initial

SHARPENING AN AXE

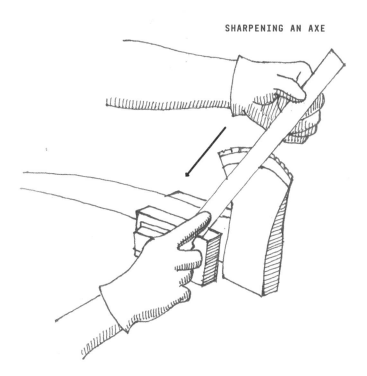

filing, and settle in, because this process should take hours of honing.

The finishing touch on your blade involves a circular whetstone, and a little bit of linseed oil. The oil, when applied conservatively to the whetstone, floats metal particles off of the axe. The motion used with the whetstone is similar to "wax-on" (you'll be ready for the All Valley

SHARPENING AN AXE
continued

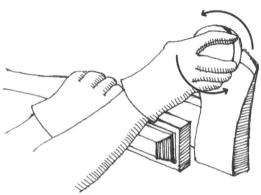

Karate Tournament in no time). Circular movements concentrated close to the arc of the blade should create a "fanned" effect on the bit. The mark should look like an arc about three inches from the blade on a "flat-ground" axe, or ½-inch chisel for your average hardware store blade.

BE SURE YOUR BLADE IS SHARP. Check the axe head to make sure it won't come flying off mid-swing. Inspect the handle to make sure there aren't any cracks or potential splits. Wear steel-toed boots as well. Also, be sure your tree doesn't fall on you or anyone else. Carefully consider the landing of the tree and your escape route as the tree is falling.

RE-HANDLING AN AXE

Congratulations, you have earned your flannel shirt! And now you have a loose or broken axe handle to show for it. One temporary fix for a wobbly axe head is to hammer a couple of nails into the eye. These nails will cause the wood to expand, while the head will stay put for a little longer. However, replacing the haft will be inevitable.

Axes tend to snap between the neck and shoulders. The biggest challenge is knocking the broken wood out of the eye. It usually takes a few whacks from a hammer and chisel, but if needed, you can loosen the wood with a few stabs of a power drill. Sawing off the handle first can help as well. After knocking out the broken piece, your axe head should be completely free of its old handle.

You will need:

- A new handle (store-bought or handmade)
- A thin wooden wedge for your kerf
- Carpenter's glue

① Once you've selected your new axe handle, you will need to make a kerf. Placing the handle into the eye, wiggle the handle through until it's out on the other side. If the handle sticks out of the top of the head a little bit, that's okay. Mark the bottom of the axe head with a pencil, then remove the head from the handle. Saw from the top into the handle down to your line, making your kerf.

❷ Put the handle through the eye again, adjusting as needed. Using a blunt object to strike it through can help.

RE-HANDLING AN AXE

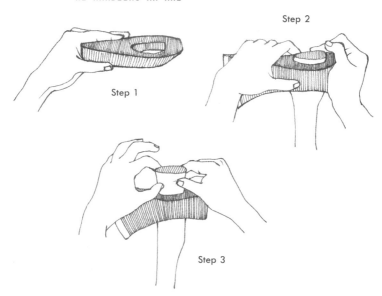

Step 2

Step 1

Step 3

❸ Stuff the wooden wedge into the kerf to the top of the head and handle. Tap it into place with a blunt object. Then secure this with glue. You can hammer in metal wedges to help in securing it, as well as adding more glue where the eye meets the handle.

❹ Once the glue is dry, saw off any remaining bits protruding from the top of the axe head, such as excess handle or the wooden wedge.

Out with the old, in with the new.

According to the National Interagency Fire Center, an average of 72,000 wildfires burn throughout the United States per year.

STACKING FIREWOOD

It's often said that firewood warms the body in three ways: the labor of splitting, the work of stacking, and finally the burning of what you toiled for. Seeing the firewood finished and stacked neatly in tower or silo shapes, we feel warm in a different way. To quote Henry David Thoreau, "Every man looks at his wood-pile with a kind of affection. I loved to have mine before my window, and the more chips the better to remind me of my pleasing work."

The process of stacking and keeping seasoned wood dry at home involves little more than a shed. However, for those without a shed or a rack, effective stacking techniques are simple. It's important to keep ventilation in mind when putting each piece of wood in place. Firewood, when kept outside in the elements, should be uncovered and spaced a couple inches apart. For stable piles, each log when stacked against the other should correspond in shape.

TOWERS

Somewhat like setting up a game of Jenga, building a tower stack is ideal for fuelwood that is short in length (especially helpful for making solid ends to your pile). Stack three pieces side by side, but with a couple inches of breathing room. Then, stack another layer of three perpendicularly, and continue this pattern until it reaches to chest level. Continue building these towers until you get a pile of wood that resembles a **cord** (eight feet long, four feet high, three feet deep). You can cover the top with a tarp, but don't completely cover it. This lets the wood dry out and keeps it from collecting condensation under plastic.

TOWER

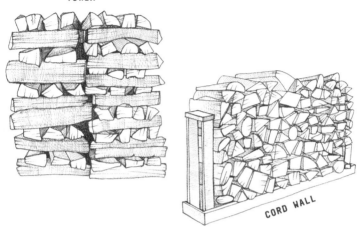

CORD WALL

CORD WALL

A little more straightforward than building a tower, a cord wall is exactly what the name suggests. Find a place alongside your house that gets plenty of sunlight, preferably so that the wood can be laid out from east to west. Then, begin setting your wood perpendicularly to the wall. The advantage of this stacking method is the efficient use of space combined with ease of removing the wood when it's time for a fire.

One cord equals 128 cubic feet of wood.

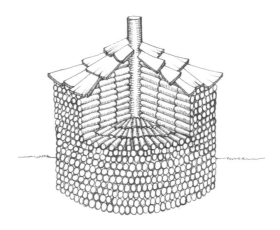

SHAKER-STYLE

Also known as the Holz Hausen method, this method of creating a circular woodpile takes a little more calculation. Your wood should be equal in height and width, so start with creating a circle with your firewood equal to the height you think the end result will be. Start by forming a ring with your chopped wood. Add layer upon layer, raising the walls as if each piece of wood were a brick for a humble home. Fill the center of the ring with uneven pieces of wood—these will prop up the "roof" of your shaker-style pile.

Once you have finished fortifying the walls of your silo-shaped stack of wood, you can top off the pile and shape it like a cone. Use a tarp to cover only the top, and use extra pieces of wood to weigh the tarp down.

HAULING

Chopping is one thing. Hauling those sweet-smelling chunks of birch to a dry place is another, laborious story. If your aim is to produce a cord of firewood, you would need to yield close to 200 pieces. A full cord—measured as four feet wide, four feet deep, and eight feet long—weighs at least 4,000 pounds, or more if it's green. That's heavier than a midsize car. A face cord is also four feet wide and eight feet long, but isn't as deep, usually sixteen to eighteen inches deep.

Hauling an entire cord of firewood is no easy task, either for a midsize car or a full-size pick-up truck. Before trying to load up your truck with firewood, it's important to take measurements, and consider this: *How much wood could a wood truck truck if a wood truck could truck wood?* The answer is half of a cord if you drive a full-size pickup truck with three cubic yards and a depth of almost two feet in the bed. A short-bed pickup can carry up to a third of a cord—but that's pushing it. To be on the safe side, make sure you know your truck's payload capacity. When you overload the bed of your truck, you unload the front, which can inhibit proper steering. If you already make a habit of loading your bed with a couple thousand pounds of wood every month, be sure to keep an eye on the wear and tear of your shocks, suspension, and rear axle.

THE GOOD WOOD

Bear in mind that the right wood calls for the right situation. Maybe you're looking for wood that crackles, pops, and sparks like well-timed sound effects to your ghost story. Or maybe wood that splits most compliantly with your axe. Maybe you're looking for most heat per log, or something that burns all night in the hearth. Or maybe you're looking for the smell of citrus, cinnamon, sage, or malt.

So much depends upon the wood you choose. Whatever wood you go with, make sure it's well seasoned. Seasoning, which requires six months to a year of drying out firewood, gets rid of moisture dwelling in the grains, which could cause smoke to form creosote in a chimney.

BRITISH THERMAL UNIT (BTUS) measure the amount of work needed to raise the temperature of one pound of water to 1 degree Fahrenheit. To put this in perspective, a kitchen match generates 1 BTU, whereas a cord of firewood ranges between 10 and 24 million BTUs.

Alder firewood is straight-grained and splits with ease. They burn best when seasoned and quickly. Overall, alder is a decent choice for campfires and cabins for its sweet smell and for its fast growth.

Grade: B-

17.5 million BTUs per cord

Ash is classic and trusty firewood. The white ash is perhaps the most commonly used firewood, coming from deciduous forests, and burns when green. It lasts long into the night as well.

Grade: A

21.6 million BTUs per cord

Beech grows its silver-gray bark in deciduous forests east of the Mississippi. Its extremely dense wood takes time to catch fire but burns cleanly without much sparking.

Grade: A+

22.7 million BTUs per cord

Birch grows in the coldest deciduous forests of the Northern Hemisphere, across Scandinavia, North America, and Siberia. People living in these regions depend on birch's dense fuelwood, water-resistant properties, and flammable and oily bark.

Grade: B+

19.5 million BTUs per cord

Cedar makes for great tinder and kindling. The soft, splintery, and porous wood catches easily, with loud pops and crackles—so give burning cedar some room.

Grade: A-

11.6 million BTUs per cord

Douglas fir, always associated with the Christmas tree, makes for fantastic, loud-popping kindling—especially for festive beach bonfires on New Year's Day after your tree has long gone dry in the living room. Just be warned that the sap-laden trunk and fragrant needles make for a very flammable holiday ornament.

Grade: B+

17.4 million BTUs per cord

Elm, though one of the most aesthetically beautiful hardwoods, is a notoriously difficult wood to split, saw, or chop. Why waste good elm when you can make a coffee table with knotty interlocking grains?

Grade: B+

19.5 million BTUs per cord

Oak, with the 90 different species that occur in the United States, has mixed reviews for burning. It takes a long time to season, and the wood, similarly to the elm, is extremely dense and labor-intensive for splitting. Oak is better suited for

Grade: B+

22.5 million BTUs per cord

deflecting cannonballs and lining hulls of frigates like the USS *Constitution* (which was nicknamed "Old Ironsides" for a reason).

Pine works well for campfires with its snapping, sparking, and scent; however, it can be dangerous to burn indoors. Creosote build-up in chimneys is a huge drawback to burning a citrusy, but resin-rich cord of pine. Pine splits into kindling and catches fire with ease and is best suited for a night of camping in alpine country.

Grade: B

15.3 million BTUs per cord

Sugar maple, which puts on pageantry of blazing red leaves during the fall, keeps a good fire long through the winter. Caramelizing scents make maple excellent firewood for a wood stove or cabin.

Grade: A

24 million BTUs per cord

Walnut might be too exquisite for firewood. But with its medium-hard density and malty aroma, it makes great, long-lasting fuel.

Grade: A

20 million BTUs per cord

CHAPTER 2

FOR THE HOME

O FOR A MUSE OF FIRE, THAT WOULD ASCEND THE BRIGHTEST HEAVEN of INVENTION.

-WILLIAM SHAKESPEARE

CABINS EVOKE THE HUMBLE BEGINNINGS of American self-reliance. Lincoln's childhood home, Thoreau's cabin at Walden Pond, and the secluded log house you found on Airbnb share a common bond: a fireplace or stove to stir the walls with radiating heat. Even a rundown hunting shed in the middle of nowhere can feel like a mansion with the simple splendor of a fire going.

What kind of a cabin doesn't have a fireplace, you ask? No cabin. No cabin at all. Maybe a cabin built on a Hollywood set, or one with a wimpy gas, electric, or pellet fireplace. The lack of a real fireplace means you dwell in a Lincoln Log of Lies.

WHAT A FIRE NEEDS

At the most basic level, a fire consists of three building blocks: oxygen, fuel, and heat. Combine these elements with an exothermic chain reaction and *voila,* you have a flame.

The fuel for this book is exclusively the combustible material native to the place you are in: birch, cedar, twigs, dried grass, or even yak dung. Burn what you can burn in good conscience. Using accelerants like lighter fluid may be great for getting barbecues off and running, but using lighter fluid for starting fires in a fireplace is not only unnecessary but also risky—not to mention wimpy. Every year the American Burn Association reports that over 6,000 barbecuers—especially while drinking—end up severely burned from lighter fluid accidents. So for the purpose of building fires, we recommend using sticks and kindling for our fuel.

The oxygen needed for your fire is in the crisp alpine air where you're camped, or in the wind whistling over the chimney top on a winter's night. In each section of this book, you'll learn how to optimize the ventilation of your chimney, hearth, or fire ring without choking your fire or leaving it too exposed.

Heat, the third facet of the triangle, is initiated by an exothermal chain reaction. A bow drill grinding into soft wood, sparks flying from a hunting knife against an iron striker, a match bursting into phosphorescent light—these actions create heat from friction and (if you do it right) react with combustible materials and oxygen to make fire. And hopefully by the end of this book, you will be able to make fire in any weather and any condition.

TYPES OF FIRES

Putting out a fire is never as simple as throwing a bucket of water onto flame. In fact, water can worsen an out-of-control fire depending on its fuel source. Different classes of fires require different extinguishing agents.

FLAMMABLE LIQUIDS

Petroleum gasoline, ethanol, paint, and other flammable liquids can be put out by an opposing chemical chain reaction. **DON'T** use water to put out these fires. Instead, use a dry chemical extinguisher. This multipurpose fire extinguisher does the job on most fires, so it's good to have one in the kitchen or garage. These extinguishers stop the exothermal reaction with an agent that blocks the exchange between oxygen and fuel.

GREASE FIRES

The kitchen is a common place for spontaneous, uncontrolled fires to jump from a pan or oven. If it's a grease fire, use baking soda. **CAUTION:** Splashing water onto a grease fire is the worst thing you can do. Water separates from oil immediately, which causes scalding grease to splatter.

Here are some steps to put out a grease fire:

❶ Turn off the burner. There is potential of burning oil splattering and contacting your skin, so be advised not to move the pan.

❷ If the fire is small, smother it with baking soda. The chemical properties of baking soda ($NaHCO_3$) allow for the powder to release carbon dioxide when in contact with a flame. Baking soda is also a product in fire extinguishers.

❸ If the fire is larger (i.e., coming from a deep fryer), cover the pan with a metal lid to smother the flames.

Wildfires are endemic in states west of the Mississippi river. In the early 1970s, fire season in the west typically lasted for five months. Today, fire seasons continue through seven months.

PREPARING YOUR FIRE

The parenting proverb, "I brought you into this world, and I can take you out" rings true here too. Fire is a tiny life that must be kept alive, and the responsibility of keeping the fire going rests squarely on the shoulders of its creator. Fire requires constant attention, maintenance, and a steady diet of fuel. The signs of a struggling fire, like heavy smoke, should elicit an almost motherly response in the fire tender. Caring for the fire means having a poker, shovel, and brush within arm's reach. These tools allow the tender to shift logs, agitate coals, sweep ash, and dispose of the excess remains.

- fire poker
- tongs
- shovel
- brush

Shoveling Ash

Thou see'st in me the glowing of such fire,
Where on the ashes of his youth doth lie,
As the deathbed whereon it must expire,
Consumed with that which it was nourished by.
—Shakespeare, Sonnet 73

Evidently, Shakespeare knew that too much ash can suffocate a fire. Make much ado about clearing out the remains of the previous fire by scooping out the excess ash from the bottom of the fire grate to create airflow. Before disposing of the remains into your green waste bin, first make sure the ash is cool to touch and that there are no glowing coals, perhaps even disposing the ash in a metal can just in case.

Make sure your damper is open. It looks like a thin metal plate with a hinge connected to the chimney. Use the lever to open the damper to keep the flow of smoke traveling upward through the chimney, rather than filling the living room with smoke. The correct way of using a

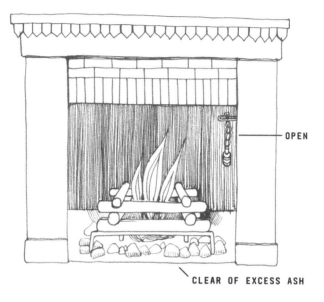

OPEN

CLEAR OF EXCESS ASH

damper is to open it completely as you're getting your fire started. Then, when the fire is off and roaring, lower the damper a few notches until the lack of airflow weakens the fire and smoke begins to collect. Open the damper notch-by-notch until the smoking ceases.

Stuff the bottom of the grate.

Stuff with day-old newspapers, cardboard, or pages from an old phonebook. But magazines or glossy paper don't burn well and only add smoke and toxic fumes to the process.

Set starter wood in the center of the grate. Start small, and use splintery pieces of kindling to make a foundation to the little log cabin you're about to construct. Lay three pieces of kindling down, spaced apart by an inch. Then add another layer of kindling perpendicularly to make a second layer.

Add larger pieces of kindling. Continue building your log cabin using three to four pieces of kindling for each layer. Remember to leave room for ventilation.

Get the fire going with a single match. With a sturdy log cabin ready to burn on top of your fire grate, set a match on multiple edges of the newspaper underneath. The flames should travel across the tinder-paper with ease. The flames will travel upward from the newspaper, catch splinters in the kindling, and spread upward.

Adjust the fire with tongs or a poker. Fires don't always begin in perfect health. Smoking furiously or dwindling early sends a message to the fire tender that adjustments need to be made. Use these wrought-iron tools to move your kindling with slight adjustments so as not to ruin the structure. A dwindling fire that hasn't caught the kindling means you must add more tinder; plumes of smoke mean you must create more space between the kindling.

WOOD-BURNING STOVES

While fireplaces are aesthetically pleasing, wood-burning stoves have a few more advantages. First invented in the mid-sixteenth century, stoves are space heaters and cook tops all in one, cast-iron contraption. Old models of stoves are definitely contributors to poor air quality, especially for launching soot and carbon dioxide into the atmosphere. However, newer EPA-approved wood stoves have improved so much in design that they make less of an environmental impact than fireplaces, which pump out CO_2 gases eight times more than an EPA-approved stove.

Wood stoves obviously aren't for everyone. To some, they're ugly, they insist on being front and center of the room, and they burn anyone who accidentally touches the stove. Yet stoves undeniably share a common trait with the campfire—the warmth draws us in.

ALTERNATIVES TO BURNING WOOD

Smoke generated from burning firewood contains carbon monoxide, nitrogen oxides, soot, and fine particles that can affect people with breathing difficulty. And there's an obvious dilemma for environmentally conscious people who still want to get a fire going on a winter's night. Lars Mytting, author of the exquisite manual *Norwegian Wood*, cites that for every two pounds of wood burned in a stove, four pounds of CO_2 gets released into the atmosphere.

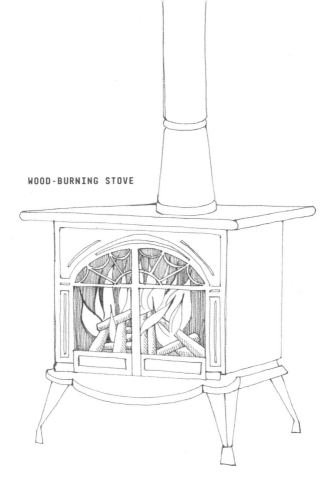

WOOD-BURNING STOVE

However, he rationalizes that the release of CO_2 from the wood—burned or left to rot—is inevitable anyways. And a tree spends its lifetime absorbing carbon dioxide, only to release it at the end of its life, which is then taken up by new trees through burning.

In some parts of the world, wood isn't readily available to chuck into the stove. In the Himalayan regions of Nepal, for example, yak dung is a central source of fuel for stoves. Similarly in the States, natives of the Great Plains used buffalo patties to burn for warmth and cooking. And stoves are best for burning dry animal poop for obvious sanitary reasons.

Aside from animal dung, there are plenty of other alternatives to wood that can power a stove. Alcohol, electricity, and wood pellets (compacted saw dust and other wood byproducts) in a pellet stove or with a fireplace insert are also green alternatives to firewood. Even used up coffee grounds can be compacted into fuel. If these options do not work for you and your family, be sure to check the fireplace for drafts, cracks, and leaks, and sweep the chimney to cut back on air pollution.

CLIMATE CHANGE, by driving up temperatures, has increased the chances of wildfires. According to data from the Union of Concerned Scientists, average temperatures have raised 1.9 degrees Fahrenheit since 1970. Warmer temps cause snowpack in alpine country to melt earlier and earlier each year. As a result, forests become drier over the course of a warmer-than-usual summer.

DIY BACKYARD FIRE PIT

1 Before you build a fire pit, it's important to familiarize yourself with the local laws in regards to the property.

2 Avoid having your fire pit under tree branches. Find an open space in your yard, where you can look up every once in a while from the flames to see open sky.

3 A fire pit ought to be four or five feet in diameter, and a foot deep. To build your own fire pit, all you need to do is dig these dimensions and line the rim with bricks.

4 Cover the bottom of the pit with bricks, creating a dry hearth for your fire. This also creates a barrier between your wood and the damp soil beneath the bricks.

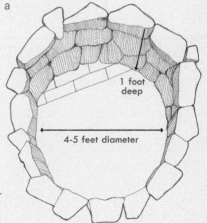

1 foot deep

4-5 feet diameter

5 Pour decomposed granite over the bricks, set your logs, and there it is. Beautiful, ain't it?

CHAPTER 3

FOR CAMPGROUNDS

How Glorious
A Greeting
the sun Gives
the Mountains!

—JOHN MUIR

WE STEP INTO THE PAST when we camp around fire. When we converse, eat meals and hold each other with a fire nearby, we re-enact a nightly human ritual performed since the beginning of our species. Camping–taking temporary residence among the Sequoias, in an arena of mountains, or on a high desert plain–brings us closer to our self-reliant selves: that we belong here.

The act of building a fire affirms this sense of belonging in the wild. Yet our cleverness with building fire can delude us into believing we have dominion over wilderness–that by rubbing wood together, we can somehow control nature. This kind of delusion is partly to blame for wildfires that decimate millions of acres a year of private property, federal land, parks, and wilderness.

Bad campfire practices can also bring invasive species that can destroy native flora and fauna. The emerald ash borer is one such invasive insect that hides in cords of firewood brought in from out of town, and has destroyed tens of millions of ash trees in twenty-four states. This is why campgrounds insist that campers buy their wood from stores within the park.

As a camper, your priority should be to leave the place in a better condition than it was before you arrived. Only after checking with the visitor center and familiarizing yourself about burn conditions and regulations should you think about building a fire.

BEFORE BUILDING YOUR FIRE

Start small. You must have your materials dry, organized, within arm's reach, and ready to receive your ember. Three components: tinder, kindling, and fuelwood. If prepared right, your ball of tinder should ignite with a spark.

TINDER

Pine needles. Birch bark. Dry leaves. The lint in your pocket. These form the fluffy, stringy cradle for your fire to thrive in and consume. A good tinder ball should resemble a bird's nest in both structure and purpose: fine, intertwined, and supporting a tiny life. The more strings in a bundle of dried grass, the more surface area for the flames to spread. Without a reliable tinder ball, you have no nexus between the tiny red glow of a coal and kindling.

To prepare your tinder ball, find any of the following:

- Dried grass
- Dead leaves
- Pine needles
- Birch bark
- Cotton balls (and petroleum jelly or lip balm)
- Cattails
- Lint
- Toilet paper
- Tinder fungus (a horse's hoof-shaped fungus that grows on the side of a tree)

TINDER FUNGUS

FEATHER STICKS are twigs or pieces of wood that catch fire more easily. Taking a knife, make curling cuts and splinters into the wood, while leaving these hanging. The result is a stick resembling feather, modified to be more flammable.

KINDLING

While a tinder ball should be the size of a fist, kindling should be the size of a finger, and the length from fingertip to elbow. Starting with the smallest, most slender pieces of kindling you can build two tried-and-true structures: **tee-pee** and **log cabin**.

Building a **tee-pee** simply involves propping up a bundle of sticks to form a cone that will house your ball of tinder. Once the tee-pee is freestanding, add bigger pieces of kindling around the cone for fortification. Cracks between the pieces of kindling ensure that the fire has ventilation. Be sure to make an entrance in the tee-pee for your tinder ball. After you give it a few full-cheeked blows, the tinder ball will be engulfed in flames, which will carry upward to the cone of sticks.

The other method, **log cabin**, requires the same type of assembly as a game of Jenga. Like the tee-pee, the log cabin must have a doorway for the tinder to be inserted.

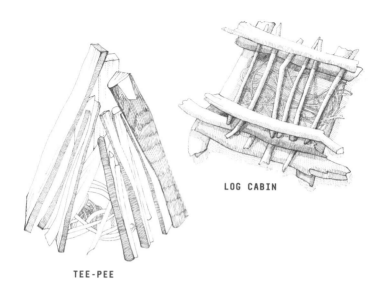

LOG CABIN

TEE-PEE

Using three to four logs at a time, stack them three layers high in a crosshatch pattern, beginning with the smallest, hairiest ones.

Dead pine trees tend to have a wealth of flammable wood made so by the sap and tar pooling at the base of the decaying tree. **PITCHWOOD**, also called fat wood or grease wood, is harvested from the stumps of these dead pines.

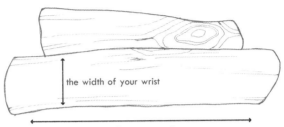

the width of your wrist

from fingertip to elbow

FUELWOOD

The same way fire jumps from tinder to kindling, fuel-wood requires kindling for enough heat and surface area. Fuelwood is the cherry on top. At least the width of your wrist, and the length from fingertip to elbow, these logs keep the fire popping and cracking through the night.

THE WILDERNESS ACT OF 1964 recognizes wilderness as "an area where the earth and its community of life are untrammeled by man, where man himself is a visitor who does not remain."

GETTING THE SPARK

Thumbstrike. If you can snap your fingers, then you can light a match with nothing but the edge of a fingernail. Using a strike-anywhere match, lighting a match with a thumbnail can be useful if you don't have a good enough striking surface. Take a match and curl your index finger tightly around it, leaving only the tip of the match uncovered. Then, place your thumbnail on the tip of the match, building tension between the thumbnail and the magnesium head until your thump flicks outward. The friction and quick strike of your thumbnail against the match should create a chain reaction to make the match flare up.

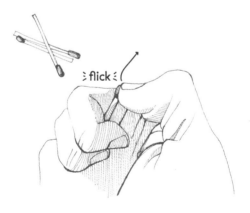

Fire By Friction. The crudest and most laborious form of making fire involves rubbing sticks against wood. The **hand drill** (pg. 102) requires the least amount of accessories, yet requires the most amount of work. The **fire plough** (pg. 106) is similar to the hand drill in its simplicity, but requires different movement. If you don't have blisters forming on your palms, then you aren't doing it right.

Strike-a-Light. With a knife, scrape the blade along a ferrocerium striker. When this happens, the blade shaves off particles of iron that oxidize from the heat caused by violent friction. Pressed against a ball of tinder, shaving sparks into the bundle can be frustrating and time-consuming task—especially if the air is moist or the tinder ball isn't stringy enough to catch a spark. For some assistance with the flame, use magnesium or other alkaline earth metals. Sparks contacting shavings of magnesium immediately burst into flames, even in wet conditions.

2015, AFTER BEING THE HOTTEST YEAR ON RECORD, set a dangerous precedent for wildfires. Over 10 million acres of private and public land went up in flames across the West.

CAMPFIRE RINGS

Fire brings out the radical individualist in us. With a campfire going, we sound our barbaric *Yawps!* or we tell stories about the land to our little ones. Few activities affirm your human independence quite like building your own fire with your bare hands on a cold night. It's no surprise that such stirring feelings of independence are immediately doused when the word *regulation* appears.

As much as we hope to be survivors like Edward Abbey or Beyoncé, we must keep in mind the rules and regulations that keep our forests intact and green. Our tax money goes to the conservation efforts of our National Parks and Monuments, State Parks, BLM land, and wherever else we set wilderness aside for public good. Illegal campfires—fires built outside of park-designated rings, or built during seasons of extremely high fire danger—threaten these public goods and the land surrounding it. One of the most expensive wildfires in history ($200 million in damages) raged through Big Sur's Joshua Creek Ecological Preserve because of an illegal campfire.

Most campsites in National Parks, State Parks, and Bureau of Land Management (BLM) land will have designated spots for campers to light fires. The presence of a campfire ring rules out any other notion to build a fire outside of one (or build your own ring). And if there is no fire ring at your campsite, it's safe to assume that camp-fires are probably prohibited.

Park rangers and forestry officials chose these rings at campsites for a reason. Usually constructed with an iron band, fire rings are built away from trees and under-ground roots.

There are some areas—like patches of BLM high desert, or along the Pacific Northwest coast, or elsewhere—that may allow construction of your own fire ring. These areas will almost always be beaches or desert. Consider carefully the season, your proximity to neighbor-hoods, and the ease at which you can put out your fire.

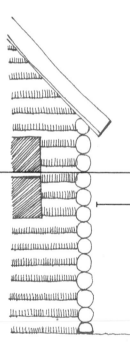

- If your campsite allows you to construct a fire ring, find a clearing fifteen feet away from trees, tree roots, and two hundred feet from any road or hiking trail. Check that the area is clear of any debris or other flammable objects, and that the fire will be built on bare soil, gravel, or sand.

- Dig a pit about a foot or so deep, and two to three feet in diameter. Ring the pit with dry rocks or stones (wet rocks will explode when heated up).
- *Voila,* you made a fire ring!

For added comfort, find some rocks or use extra pieces of wood to build benches around the fire.

FIRE RING SAFETY

200 feet from a road or trail

10 feet from a structure

7 feet from a person

15 feet from trees

1 feet deep

3 feet across

GENERAL CAMPGROUND PROTOCOLS

- Unless you're venturing out into backcountry with a wilderness permit, camp only in the places specifically marked as a campsite.
- Quiet hours are between 10 pm and 6 am.
- Park your cars, RVs, or trailers in the designated parking spots provided by the campground.
- Camping for over two weeks at one spot is usually not allowed.
- Familiarize yourself with the fire restrictions at your campsite. Buy firewood locally and pay attention to forest fire warnings.
- Fires can only be built within rings or with camp stoves.
- Make sure your fire is completely out! Douse the embers with water and smother it with ash if needed.
- Fireworks aren't allowed.
- Don't chop, hack, or deface any trees—especially for firewood. In fact, foraging for firewood is completely prohibited.
- Leave no trace.

RESPECT THE FIRE RING. Some parks have a curfew for campfires. Camp 4 in Yosemite, for example, only allows campfires until 10 pm. If you must put your fire out, the simple protocol is to pour water onto the embers or smother it with dirt and ash. Just don't pee on the fire. Please, please, *please* don't pee on your fire. That is absolutely the worst. Think about it: campgrounds are a public place. Urinating in public is obviously illegal, so it should be common sense not to do so publicly…on a public fire ring…designated for public use. Plus, the fire pit ends up smelling like your pee for a long time, especially in more arid environments. Ew. Just don't do it.

BURN SAFE

There's more to fire than keeping warm. Fire can signal rescue (see the For Survival chapter that starts on page 95), purify water, cook game, and ward off critters entering your territory. Especially in a survival situation, fire can also deliver a much-needed psychological boost: If you can make a fire, you can survive.

Unless you are thrust into survival mode, only build fires in designated campgrounds or regions where open fires are permitted. Patches of desert designated by the BLM allow for some campfires; a dry, arid environment of sage and sand can't burst into flames the way Yosemite's yellow pines do. In fact, most of our National Parks and

S'MORES DONE RIGHT

S'mores are the greatest treat ever made, for indoors and around the campfire. Ever. There is no debate. Though there are several deviations to making s'mores, the ritual remains sacred: roasting the marshmallow to your liking, taking a graham, and half of a chocolate bar, and sandwiching the ingredients in one gooey masterpiece.

HOW TO MAKE THE PERFECT S'MORE:

1. Pick a stick that measures your own arm's length, and smooth out the tip and extraneous branches with a pocketknife.

2. Spear a marshmallow with the stick. If you want to slow-cook your mallow, hold it high above the flame. For the less patient roasters, hold your mallow closer to the center of the fire.

3. Place half of a chocolate bar on top of one of your graham crackers, and keep them in close proximity to the fire ring so the chocolate will melt on the graham cracker.

4. This final step takes finesse: When your marshmallow is sufficiently toasted, pitch it with the two graham crackers to pull it from the end of your stick.

PRO TIP: If your mallow bursts into flames, DO NOT wave it around to put the flame out. A burning mallow can easily fling off the end of your stick, and land on someone's clothes or skin like sugary napalm, causing serious burns. Instead, simply blow the fire out—and if it's too charred for your liking, give it to someone who likes mallows *bien cuit*.

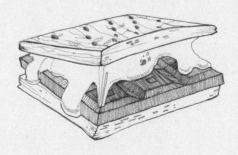

designated Wilderness Areas outlaw backcountry campfires during the dry seasons, and for good reason. Over forty-one million acres of wildland in the United States burned to a crisp between 2011 and 2016. And unfortunately many of those forest fires were caused by illegal campfires.

So before building the fire, think carefully about the consequences of a campfire gone wrong. Be sure to do the following first:

- Clear a small area that's a safe distance from overhanging branches or dead trees.
- The fire should be close to your shelter, but not too close. For example, a polyester tent should have at least ten feet of breathing room from a fire (all it takes is a spark for those things to turn into a plastic soup). If you're in a lean-to, build your small fire within an arm's length of the shelter's opening to stay insulated.
- Consider how you are going to put it out. Putting out the fire is crucial when readying to leave a campsite site or turn in for sleep.
- Douse the embers with water or smother them with topsoil. Just make sure that before leaving, the fire pit is cool to touch.

INVASIVE SPECIES

All National Parks have a strict credo when it comes to firewood: "Buy it where you burn it." Bringing foreign wood to burn in a carefully preserved habitat is not only against National Park regulations, but also it can lead to an invasion of pests and diseases, subsequently causing the deaths of hundreds of millions of trees. Invasive species included the emerald ash borer, bark beetle, Asian long-horned beetle, or the gypsy moth.

Their invasion happens when their shelters inside the firewood get too hot for their liking. So they move out of the firewood and make their new homes in nearby trees. These pests, along with alpine drought and an increasingly warming climate, leave a wake of dead wood and standing tinder just waiting to flare up in a wildfire.

Other invaders come in the form of pathogens and diseases that can bring a thriving forest to its knees. As a consequence of careless campers, these invaders have already begun to disfigure our prized wilderness areas. So remember to always buy firewood from park-sponsored stores to avoid ruining the habitat of your favorite wild getaway.

Emerald ash borer (EAB). Public enemy number one, the emerald ash borer has killed tens of millions of ash trees. They do the most damage at larval stage, engorging themselves on an ash tree's insides. At its current rate of infestation, EAB could potentially hollow out as many as seven billion ash trees and cause $10 billion in damage by 2019.

Gypsy moth. A New England species invading the Pacific Northwest, gypsy moths love devouring drought-stricken deciduous forests. For such a colorful name, these moths remove over 170,000 acres of splendid autumn foliage every year.

Bark beetle. Responsible for 29 million dead trees, these beetles thrive in drought conditions. While healthy trees can fight off infestations, widespread drought leaves pine and fir trees vulnerable to bark beetles, which in turn leaves these beetle-afflicted trees vulnerable to forest fires.

Asian long-horned beetle. Ever since 2008, the Asian long-horned beetle has been laying low with a 110-square-mile quarantine effort of Massachusetts' trees that amounted to $180 million. It will pop up occasionally in forests up the

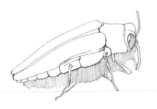

EMERALD ASH BORER

GYPSY MOTH

Eastern seaboard, destroying tens of thousands of trees in New York, before making its way into Vermont and New Hampshire.

Hemlock woolly adelgid. Descending upon 90 percent of eastern hemlocks, woolly adelgids are aphid-like insects that kill evergreens in the Appalachian range and beyond.

Beech bark disease. In the last hundred years, beech bark disease has laid waste to beech trees east of the Mississippi and into Nova Scotia. The disease starts with a beech scale insect that eats away at the tough bark, leaving it vulnerable to spores. The fungus then grows in the wounds, oozes down the tree, and weakens the foliage.

Laurel wilt. Another fungus introduced by a beetle, laurel wilt (sometimes called red bay wilt) is a death sentence to mature red bay or laurel trees native to the Southeast. Avocado trees are also vulnerable to this disease.

BARK BEETLE

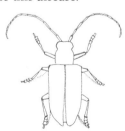

ASIAN LONG-HORNED BEETLE

Always check your wood for other pesky critters, like ants and termites, and never stack or burn infected logs near where you lay your head at night, be it house or campsite.

THE SWEDISH TORCH

Winter in Scandinavia, 1618: A few Swedish soldiers of the Thirty Years' War are huddled around a single upright log. Hands that are uncovered in a below-freezing night reach out toward sides of the log glowing red and orange.

The Swedish Torch, also called the **Canadian Candle**, is the most aesthetically pleasing, contained, and efficient way to burn with one log. First, find a suitable log that's wide enough to be split into wedges. With a hatchet, bisect the log with a few controlled chops. Don't chop straight through the middle yet, but leave the pieces connected before splitting them into sections. The end result should give you six to eight pie slices out of your log. Eight delicious pie slices. But don't think about pie right now. Think about gathering tinder.

Next, put the pieces back together, but leave breathing room for the tinder you've gathered and placed within reach. The spaces between each wedge should be stuffed and overflowing with dry tinder. Birch bark, dry pine needles, pieces of pinecone–anything to fill the gaps–and ignite. As the logs catch, fan the flames, blow, and adjust the wedges to ensure healthy oxygen flow.

SWEDISH TORCH

In snowy conditions, you may need to dig into the snow until you hit dirt. If the snow is too deep and requires too much effort, stomp out a flat surface for your fire about three feet in diameter. Then, thump each wedge in place, so that when the fire is going, the logs don't shift or tumble out of place as snow melts underneath.

WITHIN TEN MINUTES OF IGNITION, a Swedish Torch can work just as well, if not better, than that old kitchenette in your overpriced apartment. First, make a tri-pod for your pan or pot by placing stones or dense sticks on top of the candle. Much like turning the knob on a stove, you can adjust the heat by adding more tinder to the fire or moving the wedges closer or farther apart. In minutes you can have boiled water in a pot or oil bubbling in a pan. Make stir-fry, popcorn, bacon and eggs. Anything!

BONFIRES

The only thing more mesmerizing than a full harvest moon on an Indian summer night is the raging glow of a bonfire. These larger-than-life burns have been essential to celebration—breaking from the everyday, conservative cooking fire to build a decadent tower of flames. Bonfires are evanescent monuments to all that is fleeting and transient in life: the seasons, the feast day of a Saint, the funeral of Viking king. Countless cultures build these log towers, effigies, and pyres as a primitive and poignant call to celebration. Celtic Druids burned giant wicker men to the awe of their Roman occupiers. Revelers in Kyoto engage in the 500-year-old tradition of lighting bonfires in honor of their ancestral spirits during the festival of *Obon* (whence we get "bon-"). For a more recent example, look no further than Black Rock City, Nevada, where the creativity experiment, Burning Man, pops up every year.

RED TAPE
Some of the major obstacles to building bonfires have to do with the laws of the land. While burning on private property is often something you can do at your own risk, public lands have strict regulations for large bonfires—not to mention any fires built outside of a campground fire ring. So before setting up your pallets, old Christmas trees,

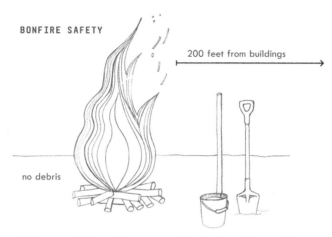

BONFIRE SAFETY

200 feet from buildings

no debris

or elaborate effigies, be sure to check the rules at the site you wish to have your burn.

Permits. For every park and public slice of land, there is a set of rules pertaining to the eco-region our government is trying to conserve. Coastal expanses, high deserts, Great Plains, and forested mountains each have unique risks for open fires. If you care about safe burning practices, make it your priority to find out which government entities manage the space: Bureau of Land Management, National Parks Service, State Park Service, and others.

What to burn. Don't burn trash, sand paper, or anything with glue, creosote, or tar.

Boundaries. Be sure to be at least 200 feet from any buildings and any flammable objects above or on the ground.

Where you are. If you're burning on a beach, be mindful of what wildlife you could be disrupting. Beach bonfires present obstacles for sea turtle hatchlings.

Leaving No Trace. Clean-up is essential to keeping bonfires a continued privilege on public land. Keep in mind the time and date on your permit for when the fire must be extinguished, and make sure your fire is completely out.

Other Tips for Controlling Your Fire

- In public campgrounds, having a small, manageable fire is imperative. Don't burn any kindling larger the length of your elbow to fingertips, and width of your wrist.
- Keep water nearby.
- Use a long stick to adjust the firewood.
- Use a spade to smother your fire with spent ashes or moist dirt.

THE STICK TAPPING RIDDLE

"Ehem. I can tap this stick just right."
Thump thump.

So goes one of the most hilarious games to play
around a campfire! To play this game—which works
as a practical joke for everyone who isn't in the
know—hold a stick in your hand and begin each
declaration with a clearing of the throat: "Ehem!"
followed by the sentence, "I can tap this stick
just right." Then, pass the stick off to the next
person to see if they were listening. Once someone
finally understands that tapping the stick "just
right" requires the "Ehem!" then you can acknowl-
edge their ability to tap the stick "just right."
And the stick travels around the campfire until
everyone, ehem, can tap the stick just right.

CHAPTER FOUR

FOR SURVIVAL

LOOK DEEP
INTO NATURE,
AND THEN YOU WILL
UNDERSTAND
EVERYTHING BETTER.

—ALBERT EINSTEIN

IT WAS SUPPOSED TO BE a simple out-and-back hike through your prized National Park, or that once-a-year hunting trip in the Idaho wilderness, or a "three-hour tour." But sure enough, you left your map in the car, or the landmarks you knew you'd see again are nowhere to be found, and now the sun is getting lower along the horizon. Then it hits you: You might be lost.

First, you should stop and take a few deep breaths. If you can retrace your steps, then do this until you're sure again. But if the sureness doesn't come, and you find yourself confounded by the mesmerizing thickets of pines and disquieting solitude, then you have a decision to make: Should I stay or should I go?

Unless you find better cellular reception on a hilltop, or a natural calamity occurs, opting to stay where you are is your best bet. In other cases, your degree of lost-ness can go deeper. Maybe you're shipwrecked on an island, or you crash-landed in the Canadian boreal forest. What else do you have to survive with but the clothes on your back and your trusty knife?

One of the first things to do when thrown into an extreme survival situation is to construct—by any means—a fire to signal Search and Rescue.

No day-tripping or over-nighting hiker should ever step out of their front doors without the commonsense tools needed to survive. You need some way of navigating yourself from your car to your destination and back to your car. You need protection from the sun and elements, the right insulation, a working headlamp, first-aid supplies, and a tent or tarp. And on a primal level, you need food, a knife, and means to build fire.

FIRE SUPPLIES FOR EVERY HIKER

Plastic Lighters. Lightweight, durable, and lasting up to 3,000 lights, these little guys are the most efficient and hands-down easiest way to make fire from little more than a bundle of dried grass and twigs. They save time, physical effort, and mental energy—three things that must be rationed if you're waiting for a rescue. Of course, nature purists and stoic survivalists like *Survivorman* host Les Stroud bristle at the convenience of a BIC lighter, and understandably so. Part of the joy of "surviving," or the recreational version of it, is overcoming hardship and the challenge of building a fire from what you foraged, not what you can buy at a gas station quick-stop. But in real, unplanned survival situations, making fire through crude means should be a last-ditch effort if there are easier ways to make fire available to you. In this situation, take the path of least resistance and use the plastic lighter in your pack.

All-Weather Matches. If you have objections to a lighter's use of accelerants or to the plastic industry, but still want

reliable means to start a fire in any situation (storms, blizzards, flash floods), then stormproof matches belong in your survival kit. Truly, this match is a masterpiece of chemistry. Striking the match on any dry surface produces a slow flare-up that turns into a violent and awesome flare of purple and blue flame, even when lit underwater. Plus these matches burn for up to fifteen seconds and it should only take one to light a tinder ball.

These matches can take a beating in the elements.

Light them in strong winds and they stay lit. Smother them in dirt—they stay lit. Dip them in water—you guessed it. The secret to making these matches so resilient is this: a wax coating that protects the highly reactive elements—red phosphorus, potassium, or magnesium—on the matchstick.

Magnesium Block. Getting a fire going with magnesium and a knife is a more difficult method than using a lighter or match, but in dry conditions it can be a quick process. This method of fire-lighting requires an expertly crafted tinder ball, a dry surface on which to place the tinder, and a back that will not spasm while you're hunched over, scraping for sparks. Most of these magnesium blocks come with an iron-based striker for your knife to brush against, creating a flurry of sparks. The goal is to connect those sparks with the shavings of magnesium. With a knife, make shavings of magnesium from the block (which are about the same size as a plastic lighter). Shave a pile of magnesium strips onto a ball of tinder until the shavings add up to a "pinch" in terms of measurement.

Then, the fun part: Find a comfortable position. Press your knife and striker into the tinder and scrape madly, aiming the sparks at your fresh-shaved alkaline metal. The flying sparks will eventually react violently with the magnesium in a tiny but sustained light. Once the magnesium

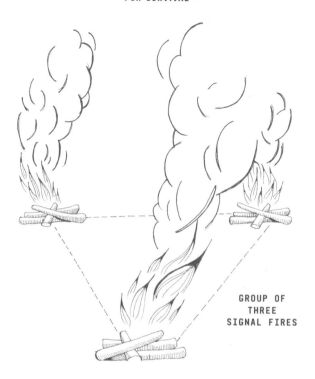

GROUP OF
THREE
SIGNAL FIRES

begins to catch fire, carefully close your tinder ball around the shavings. With small movements of your wrist, rock the bundle of burning magnesium until it begins to smoke, and continue until you have a flame.

SIGNAL FIRES

Construct your signal fire on hilltops, or in a clearing in the woods or beaches. If you are lost in the middle of the day, use material that will smoke heavily: leaves, green wood, grass–the damper the better.

Distress signals are universally a series of three. Building a group of three signal fires will not only create a larger smoke cloud but also will effectively communicate your emergency. If you have enough time, energy, or space, create an SOS or HELP out of branches.

LOW-TECH FIRE-STARTING METHODS

HAND DRILL

For stubborn folks who like doing everything the hard way, the hand drill is crude, frustrating, painful, and just for you. Two simple components give us the hand drill: the hearth board and the spindle. Coals are created when the user "drills" the spindle in a clockwise to counterclockwise motion.

So much depends upon a hand drill working. For starters, the surface on which you lay the hearth board must not be damp. Frigid temps make the process of creating a coal take longer, while a humid climate can make your life just as difficult. And altitude makes it even more difficult.

You will need:

- A fixed-blade or hunting knife
- A hearth board, dry and about 3/4-inch thick and 6 or so inches in length
- A spindle, a thin, dry stick the width of a finger, about a foot long

The Technique

❶ With your knife, cut a V-shaped notch into the edge of the hearth board, about half an inch deep. The notch creates airflow while making room for coals to collect at the base of the board. The best types of wood for the hearth board and spindle include cottonwood, aspen, willow, cedar, and cattail.

❷ The spindle should be a stick no longer than twelve to sixteen inches. Since you'll be working with your bare hands, find a stick that is smooth and stripped of bark. Any rough edges should be shaved to avoid splinters. With your knife, make a small, circular indentation for your spindle. The mark should be just enough to keep the spindle in a concentrated place.

The key to a successful spindle is the tip. A rookie mistake is to make the tip too pointed; this causes the surface area to be too small to generate enough friction for making coals. A blunt spindle, however, means increased surface area, more dust, increased friction, and less work.

③ Now the fun begins! With a boot on the edge of your hearth board, begin drilling your spindle into the wood with a back-and-forth, hand-rubbing motion. Begin slowly while applying downward force toward the hearth. As the technique catches on, increase the speed of your hands. When you reach about three inches above the base of the spindle, stop. With one hand, grab onto the spindle while the other quickly moves to the top, never releasing pressure. If you're doing it right, you'll hear squeaking sounds coming from the hearth board, and brown dust will form a ring around your spindle.

Gradually increase the speed of your hands as you start to smell burning wood. If you see smoke beginning to plume, don't stop! Keep rubbing until smoke is visible, and continue

HAND DRILL

rubbing for another ten seconds as the smoke builds.

❹ **The floating hand technique** is the most efficient way to keep the spindle going while applying pressure. The way this works is by forming a *V* with your hands with each back-and-forth rub. This keeps your hands from sliding downward, allowing for continuous movement of the spindle. The floating hand technique allows the most efficient way to apply constant pressure on the spindle and coals forming at the base of the hearth board.

5 To make life easier, add paracord or a boot string to the drill. Carve a groove into the top of the spindle that will serve to hold the string in place. Make loops for your thumbs about four inches apart, and place the middle of the string into the groove at the top of the spindle. With the string in place, you can apply constant pressure without taking your hands off the spindle.

THE EPA CONSIDERS WILDFIRES "'unplanned, unwanted wildland fire[s]' in forests, shrubland, and grassland, where 'the objective is to put the fire out.'"

FIRE PLOUGH

The plough method is another fire-starting technique involving wood against wood. Similar to the hand drill, the plough requires hard wood rubbing into soft wood, and grinding dust into a burning coal. The technique, however, requires a bigger stick and hearth board.

You will need:

- A fixed-blade or hunting knife
- A plough stick, a dry, sturdy stick, long enough to be gripped by two hands
- A hearth board, about 2 inches thick and tube-shaped

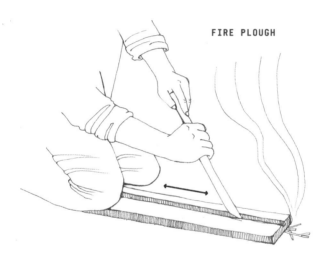

FIRE PLOUGH

The Technique

1. Choose a dry piece of wood for your hearth board, which should be about two inches thick and long enough to be held steady with a knee. Similarly to the hand drill's hearth board, carve a V-notch that will allow airflow and an outlet

for coals. The hearth board should have soft, splintery wood for the hard wood to pulverize.

❷ Unlike the hand drill, the plough stick should be slightly pointed to avoid snapping as pressure and speed are increased. The plough should be long enough to be gripped with two hands, and strong enough to support the amount of force required to start the fire (you have to put your back into it).

❸ Start with slow movements back and forth, creating a trench in the hearth board about four inches in length, reaching to the V-notch. Have a piece of cotton or tinder at the edge of the hearth board to catch the coals.

❹ While the coal is still smoldering, place the contents into your tinder nest. Wrap the nest around the coals, like you're putting together a fire taco. Let the wind do the work, shaking the nest lightly to spread the coals or making a smoky figure eight with your arm. As smoke builds, blow gently into the nest, until flames engulf the bundle of sticks. The flaming tinder is ready to be placed under sticks for a fire.

BOW DRILL

Another method for creating fire in a crunch is the bow drill. Out of all the crude methods of building a fire with only wood-on-wood friction, the bow drill requires the least amount of energy, replacing effort with ingenuity. The bow drill is an advancement to the simple hand drill technique and adds additional tools to the process. The basic components include a thin board for the hearth and a spindle that works as the "drill."

You will need:

- A fixed-blade or hunting knife
- A spindle, a solid and thick stick, about 8 to 12 inches long
- A hearth board, a flat, dry, and soft piece of wood, about 3/4-inch thick and long enough to be held steady with your boot
- A cord, either a paracord or boot string
- A stiff, bow-shaped stick
- A cup-sized piece of wood or rock

The Technique

1. Choose the bow drill components that will demand the least amount of effort in getting a coal going. When you're collecting your

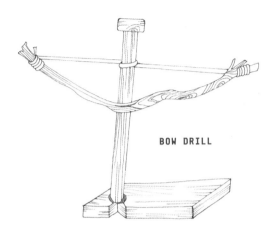

BOW DRILL

materials for the bow drill, it's important to find the driest, most effective wood you can find. The best wood to make a bow drill won't be found on the ground; look for low-hanging, dry branches in a tree. Also, find trees at the edge of clearings, or that face south in direct east-to-west sunlight. Some of the best types of wood include cedar, sumac, willow, aspen, poplar, and spruce.

While the hand drill involves a long and slender stick to bore into the wood, you should find a stick that won't snap under the weight of your hand when you're drilling full bore. Find a stick that's around eight to twelve inches at most with a solid girth. Your hearth board should be constructed from a flat, dry, and soft piece of wood, about three quarters of an inch thick and long enough to be held steady with your boot. The shape of your spindle is crucial to fire building with the bow drill. The drill itself should be shaped like a pencil: pointed on one end, rounded and blunt on the other.

Next, find your bow. Any stick with a slight arc will do—as long as it's sturdy enough to support a tense string and handle the back-and-forth work. For cord, you'll get the best results from a bootlace or paracord. (If you're stuck surviving in sandals, then you can fashion a rope from strings of green wood by braiding the strands together until you have something substantial.) Taking your knife, cut a notch on either side of your bow so as to hold the string in place. Tie a knot around each end of the bow, while keeping enough slack that it can accommodate the drill. Then, taking your drill piece, twist a loop around the stick so that the shaft is held in the middle of the bowstring.

The last component is the cup, which can be made from animal bone, rotted wood, or stone as long as it can allow both free movement of the drill and adequate pressure upon the hearth board. The cup should have a socket for the pointed end of the spindle (which performs even better when lubricated with just a little spit or sweat).

2 Once you have your bow drill assembled, take a knee or get comfortable, because this could take a while. Cut a small divot into the hearth board as you would with the hand drill, along with a V-shaped notch to give your friction fire ventilation and an outlet for your coal dust. Place a boot on your board just a few inches a way from the hole you wish to bore. Then, setting your drill bit into the divot, begin long strokes with the bow.

3 Brown dust collecting at the base of your spindle is an encouraging sign to increase speed and add pressure—but won't produce a hot coal. When you start to see fine, black dust, keep at it! If black dust and smoke start billowing from the spindle, speed up your spindle for an extra ten seconds before removing it.

PUMP DRILL

The Iroquois invented this handy method of drilling for fire that involves the use of cord. Though pump drills are brilliant stone-age inventions for creating fire and drilling through stone, they require more energy and engineering; in other words, they aren't recommended for constructing in time-sensitive survival situations. One crucial component of the pump drill is a stone weight to fix at the base of your pump drill. This takes the most time and effort to craft. Without a free weight at the base, the pump drill is useless. Built correctly, however, you can get a fire going in under a minute.

You will need:
- A fixed-blade or hunting knife
- A drill stick, made of softwood
- A weight, either made from a thin, circular rock or a circular piece of hardwood
- A cross bar, a stick of hardwood
- Cord or bootlace
- A hearth board, a flat, dry, and soft wood

The Technique

1. Take your drill stick, and bore an eyehole near the top. Thread the eye with your cord.

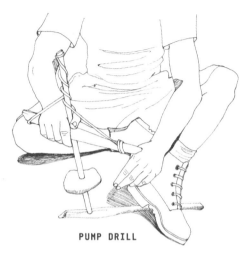

PUMP DRILL

❷ Find a circular rock of about one or two pounds or a circular piece of hardwood, and carefully carve a hole through the center with your hunting knife. Your drill should fit tightly without having the disc slip off, so measure how wide the hole should be in advance. This weight will sit toward the bottom by the pointed end of the drill.

❸ Bore a hole through the center of your cross bar stick and eyeholes on each end. Fit the drill through the middle hole, and then fasten the ends of the cord through the cross bar's eyeholes. The device should look like a cross.

④ Twist your drill stick around, so that the cord is wrapped around. The cross bar should be at the top of your drill.

⑤ Set the drill on your hearth board. Pushing down on the cross bar's handles will cause the drill and the weight to spin. The weight's mass and momentum should cause your pump to float upward while the cord recoils back around the drill's shaft. Rewind the crossbar and repeat until the friction creates fire.

SURVIVING IN THE DESERT

Somehow, you are left to survive in the hot, arid, soul-baring emptiness in the Mojave or Sonora—or pretty much anywhere in Nevada. But thank your lucky stars you came prepared with a wide-brimmed hat, sunglasses, light-colored shirt and pants that minimize sweat loss, and sunblock with a high Ultraviolet Protection Factor (UPF). You drank your fill of water before your hike and refilled it again and again before leaving the parking lot (rather than ration it like a damn fool). And you informed someone—a friend or family member—where you would be hiking, and for how long.

Good job. But now what? You can't call anyone because there isn't any cell phone service. There are no landmarks—every sagebrush or Joshua tree seems to change shape every time you look back. If you decide to return to the parking lot on a hunch, you could be walking deeper and deeper into the desert to meet your death. Stay put, and think about ways to signal for help.

FIRE FROM GLASS

If you're stranded in the desert without matches or a lighter, you may need the power of the sun to build a signal fire. Lucky for you, dry sage and dead saguaro are substantial kindling to get a modest fire going. The challenge, of course, is to harness the heat of that energy-sapping ball of fire in the sky and aim the rays at a bundle of desert-dry tinder.

If you wear glasses, then perfect. If not, then you better disassemble something that has a glass lens—maybe your watch, or a shard of a beer bottle, or even a small mirror—anything that can be held in one hand, aimed to reflect the sun's rays. However, glasses are by far the best way to get an ember.

The trick is to add a drop of water to the inside of the lens. The water creates a biconvex effect—bending the light *twice*—turning your glasses into a magnifying glass and increasing your chances of making a fire.

What to look for. Angle the glass so that the sun's light passes through and magnifies onto your pile of tinder. You will see an obvious, yellow patch of light—think of it as a very slow-working "death ray." Or if it's a mirror, refract the sun's rays until you see a "death ray" appear on your fire nest.

Keep your mirror about six inches above what you wish to combust. Adjust the space of your glass like a lens, as if to put the sunlight in focus on your target. Too far away and the light is too dispersed. Too close and your light is too concentrated.

Get comfortable, because this could take twenty minutes or longer. If you can, find shelter from the sun or cover your back, neck, and head.

SURVIVING IN SNOW AND ICE

You're post-holing through alpine country, lost in a thicket of snow-laden conifers, and sun is getting lower. If you don't have a tent or bivy sac and a sleeping bag, your chances of surviving the night without a fire are extremely low. Fire is simply a must to keep your clothing dry, your spirits up, and your body from slipping into hypothermia.

The trick to getting a fire going in the dead cold is to make it happen **in one go**. (Read Jack London's short story *To Build a Fire* to get a good understanding of this lesson.) The work of building a fire will bring temporary warmth to your body, but the evaporation of sweat, mixed with heat convection from touching cold objects, will suck the life out of you the longer you take to build your fire.

FIRE IN ICE

Pick a place for your fire that isn't directly under branches. It's so frustrating to finally have your fire going, only to have a branch drooping with snow dump its weight onto your only hope of surviving! Find a clearing that will accommodate a fire close to the opening of your lean-to, snow cave, or other improvised shelter.

Once you've found your site, tramp down the snow-pack with your boots in a 4-foot-wide circle. Then, start digging with either a shovel or your gloved hands until

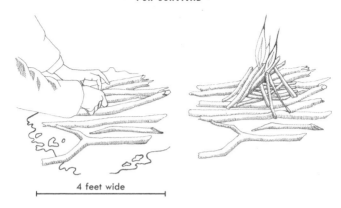

4 feet wide

you hit ice. Take your knife or hatchet, and start hacking away at the ice until you've hit dirt.

On the south side of a pine tree—a low-hanging source of fuel exposed to the sun—you'll find sticks, bark, and dry branches to use for your fire. First, find materials to make a dry bed for your tinder. Lay these materials out criss-crossed to create a dry platform above the wet ground.

Then, with your tinder and kindling close by (and out of the way from snow), construct your teepee or log-cabin with a small opening to receive your flaming ball of tinder.

SYMPTOMS OF HYPOTHERMIA INCLUDE: uncontrollable shivering, slurred speech, fatigue, drowsiness, and odd behavior. Hypothermia victims have also reported a strange burst of bodily warmth before succumbing, exposed to the cold.

NATURE'S DEFENDERS

THE SIERRA CLUB

The Sierra Club has been dedicated to the exploration, enjoyment, and preservation of wilderness ever since it was founded on June 4, 1892. The Sierra Club is a group of wilderness enthusiasts and, unsurprisingly, the nation's largest and most influential environmental organization, boasting over two million members and supporters. Founded by our favorite naturalist John Muir, the Sierra Club has accomplished many feats since then, including passing the Clean Air Act, the Clean Water Act, and the Endangered Species Act. The club has worked tirelessly to secure the protection of millions of acres of wilderness that everyone can enjoy to this day. Aside from their work to promote the enjoyment of the outdoors and the preservation of wilderness, the Sierra Club has recently been working toward the goal of moving away from the use of fossil fuels, and toward clean energy. This club wants to protect the environment, so that you can enjoy it!

THE NATURAL RESOURCES DEFENSE COUNCIL

The Natural Resources Defense Council (NRDC) cares about our planet and everything on it, from plants to people! Founded in 1970 by a group of environment adoring law students and attorneys, the NRDC consists of over two million members and online activists today, with know-how from 500 scientists, lawyers, and policy advocates worldwide. All of these passionate and intelligent people around the world are participating in the NRDC's efforts to protect the air, water, and wilderness that they believe should be accessible to everyone. This nonprofit organization covers all areas of conservation including climate change, energy, food, health, oceans, water, and the wilderness. The NRDC provides all of us living on this precious planet with tips on how to conserve and even offers examples for different ways to get involved in their fight for a cleaner planet. The NRDC is helping us help the world—no one can do it alone!

U.S. NATIONAL PARK SERVICE

The U.S. National Park Service (NPS) just celebrated its 100th birthday in 2016! Many people around the world have the U.S. National Park Service to thank for their road trip destinations, epic backpacking trips, and escapes into the mystifying nature that has been preserved on U.S. soil. The NPS protects the special places of America, which collectively gain over 275 million visitors each year. The NPS includes close to 400 areas across the United States for the enjoyment and education of anyone who pays a visit. The official emblem of the NPS, an arrowhead, is representative of the organization's historical values to conserve not only natural resources but cultural resources as well. Everyone needs to get lost in a forest at some point in life, and the NPS makes sure that forest is preserved and waiting for you!

TOP 10 NATURALISTS

1. JOHN MUIR
(April 21, 1838–December 24, 1914)

We owe the "Father of the National Parks" John Muir a big thank you for the great American wilderness we enjoy today. Muir was more than just an outdoorsman; he was a lover of all things wild and natural—and wrote on the subject often. A factory accident left Muir temporarily blinded as a young man, and after his recovery he never returned to the indoor lifestyle. His first major expedition led him on a thousand-mile hike from Indiana to the Gulf of Mexico, and, despite the sore feet, he was hooked. After that, he was most famous for his role in the establishment of the Yosemite and Sequoia National Parks. He also spearheaded the foundation of the Sierra Club, and was unanimously voted president—a role he was more than worthy of and served valiantly for twenty-two years. Muir's influence was wide-ranging, and he even took President Theodore Roosevelt camping—leading to Roosevelt's decision to designate the famous Grand Canyon as a National

Monument! John Muir made it his mission to protect our beautiful wilderness, and America's National Parks wouldn't have been the same without him.

2. THEODORE ROOSEVELT
(October 27, 1858–January 6, 1919)

Theodore Roosevelt had to have been one of our most earthy, crunchy presidents yet, and we love him for it! Without him we may have lost out on so many of our wonderful National Monuments—imagine life without the Grand Canyon! Our twenty-sixth president created the United States Forest Service (USFS) in an attempt to conserve our wilderness and promote sustainability of the country's resources. In efforts to protect wilderness and wildlife, he established 150 national forests, 51 federal bird reserves, five national parks, and four national game preserves. Needless to say, throughout his administration the National Park System gained some weight. The 1906 American Antiquities Act allowed him to bypass congressional approval to establish national monuments at his leisure—Congress couldn't get in the way of the eighteen national monuments he established. By the time Roosevelt's run in the White House was up, he had successfully protected 230 million acres of public land and made America that much more enjoyable for us!

3. HENRY DAVID THOREAU
(July 12, 1817–May 6, 1862)

Henry David Thoreau, a major transcendentalist, contributed many writings on natural history and philosophy throughout his lifetime. One of his most famous works was the book *Walden,* which echoed the importance of simple living in a natural environment. Thoreau absolutely hated the materialism that was emerging throughout his lifetime and would definitely be labeled a minimalist today, especially considering the two years he spent living in a self-built cabin on Walden Pond. He tried his hand at living the savage naturalist lifestyle that Muir pursued, but a trip to climb Mt. Katahdin proved to be a bit too lonely for his liking. Afterward, he saw nature as a place to preserve, explore, and use to fulfill his primitive instincts, but he needed refuge in the civilization of Concord—promoting a balance between the wild and the refined. Most of Thoreau's contributions as a naturalist were philosophical; his transcendentalist ideals even impacted the great John Muir.

4. RACHEL CARSON
(May 27, 1907–April 14, 1964)

Rachel Carson was a fierce lady in the field of marine biology who never stopped fighting for the environmental movement. Already an established naturalist, she was awarded the Presidential Medal of Freedom for her con-tributions in environmentalism—her book *Silent Spring* being highly influential in the cause. Her prolific writings communicated to the general public the dangers of the untested usage of pesticides and were part of the progress that led to the government ban on the use of DDT. She was the second woman to gain a full-time professional position with the Bureau of Fisheries, rising from a junior aquatic biologist to become Editor-in-Chief of all publications for the U.S. Fish and Wildlife before resigning to write full time. Carson possessed an undying love for nature and challenged society to view wilderness as vulnerable—as something we should protect.

5. ALDO LEOPOLD
(January 11, 1887–April 21, 1948)

To some, Aldo Leopold is referred to as "The Father of Modern Wildlife Conservation," so it's unsurprising that he and Muir were both key players in keeping the United States healthy and green! Leopold's career began at the U.S. Forest Service. A talented writer, he published hun-dreds of works including various essays, articles, speeches, textbooks, and even poems throughout his career. A major win in his fight for the environment was in 1924 with the creation of the Gila Wilderness Area in New Mexico—an area he had fought tirelessly for all his life! After a fulfilling career with the U.S. Forest Service, Leopold went on to take a position as a faculty member specializing in game management at the University of Wisconsin. Among all his amazing contributions, he is most famous for his book *A Sand Country Almanac,* comprised of forty-one essays. In this book he explores his famous ideology of "land ethic" and ecological conscious—essentially that we should respect every piece of the environment, from bugs to birds, because we all rely on each other.

6. MARJORY STONEMAN DOUGLAS
(April 7, 1890–May 14, 1998)

Marjory Stoneman Douglas dedicated her 108 years of life on planet Earth to protecting it. Her lifelong pursuit of activism began during the First World War, where she became involved in feminism, racial justice, and—of course—conservation. She was ahead of her times by caring for these causes, and she had a strong influence in the creation of Everglades National Park—supporting the project through her writing and by serving on the committee. Her book *The Everglades: Rivers of Grass* defined the continuing threats on the river she dedicated her adult life in protecting. She went on to write other books; however, the Everglades became a part of her identity and she even titled her autobiography *Voice of the River*, as she truly was the river's largest advocate. Douglas was awarded the Presidential Medal of Freedom at the age of 103 for her devotion to the environment and her fight for equal rights. Many know her as "Grandmother of the Glades," and we can't help be inspired by the fierceness in her fight for the environment.

7. ENOS MILLS
(April 22, 1870–September 21, 1922)

Enos Mills was hooked on nature ever since his first ascent of the 14,225-foot Longs Peak at the age of fifteen. You could say he liked what he saw as he made that same trip over three hundred times afterwards—whether as a guide or by himself. Longs Peak became a home for Mills; he had even built a summer cabin there by the time he turned sixteen years old. A few years later Mills met John Muir, and the rest was history. Muir inspired Mills to pursue his love for nature and engage in conservation activism. Mills took this advice and began the Longs Peak Inn, guiding tourists and fellow adventurers up his beloved Longs Peak. During this time he also served as the Colorado State Snow Observer, predicting spring and summer runoff. Afterward, he spent time as a government lecturer on forestry, while writing various articles and books on nature and the Estes Park area. The most lasting contribution he made was his role in the establishment of Rocky Mountain National Park in 1915.

8. WANGARI MAATHAI
(April 1, 1940–September 25, 2011)

Wangari Maathai was a serious power woman, and an advocate for sustainability. She was the first woman in East and Central Africa to attain a doctorate degree and then went on to be awarded the 2004 Nobel Peace Price. Between her degree and the Nobel Peace Prize, she had accomplished some amazing feats for the environment and society. One of these feats was the creation of the Green Belt Movement (GBM), founded to promote community-based tree planting for environmental conservation. Since the birth of this organization, GBM communities in Kenya have planted over 51 million trees. Today, GBM also promotes water harvesting, mainstream advocacy, and taking action on climate change. The years 2009–2010 were huge for Maathai. First, she was named UN Messenger of Peace, with her focus being on environment and climate change. Next, she became a trustee of the Karura Forest Environmental Education Trust. Later, she founded the Wangari Maathai Institute for Peace and Environmental Studies (WMI). She couldn't be stopped! She was dedicated to improving environmental awareness in Africa, and her impact carries on today with her amazing organizations GBM and WMI.

9. JANE GOODALL
(Born April 3, 1934)

Jane Goodall loved the wilderness from an early age. Still, when Goodall proposed to conduct her own research in Africa, many professionals doubted her survival skills. Goodall wasn't about to let some stuffy scientists get her down, so she went to begin her famous study of the Gombe chimpanzees anyway. Goodall was an unconventional lady, naming chimps Fifi, Flo, and more. But it was this unconventionality that allowed her to see the behaviors of these animals that other scientists had missed—like how they can make and use tools, which at that point was something scientists thought only humans could do. In 1977, she founded the Jane Goodall Institute for Wildlife Research, Education and Conservation, promoting field research on her cherished chimps and empowerment of individuals to protect the environment. Later on, Goodall founded the environmental and humanitarian youth program, Roots and Shoots, which now boasts almost 150,000 members in over 130 countries. She truly transformed from a survivalist living among animals to a conservationist and so much more.

10. BARACK OBAMA
(Born August 4, 1961)

When it comes to protecting the environment, Barack Obama may be the first president in recent history that has given Theodore Roosevelt a run for his money. Obama has protected an astounding 260 million acres of America's wilderness and waters. Like Roosevelt, Obama has a strong affection for the American Antiquities Act and has established or expanded 25 national monuments. We were all excited when Obama signed the Omnibus Public Land Management Act of 2009, which enabled one of the largest expansions of land and water conservation in a long, long time. We're talking two million acres of federal wilderness, thousands of miles of trails, and over 1,000 miles of rivers. Because Obama loves the planet and wants to leave it cleaner for future generations, he came up with the Clean Power Plan (with help from the Environmental Protection Agency) to attempt to limit carbon pollution from power plants. Obama hopes it will give those in the United States the tools to access clean and affordable electricity. This man has done more for our environment than can be contained in this list, and we hope he will continue his efforts after his presidency.

TYPES OF FORESTS

TROPICAL RAINFOREST

Tropical rainforests hang out around the equator, meaning they get to avoid the winter—which may seem nice but instead of snow, these forests see 100 inches of rain each year. Tropical rainforests are home to broad-leafed trees that can get to 115 feet tall, as well as ferns, vines, mosses, palms, orchids, birds, bats, monkeys, and snakes.

TEMPERATE DECIDUOUS FOREST

Temperate deciduous forests are found all over the world: Eastern United States and Canada, Western Europe and parts of Russia, China, and Japan. These forests experience all four seasons, seeing 30 to 60 inches of rain throughout the spring, summer, and fall, and receiving snow in the winter. At the base of the varied maple, oak, birch, and evergreen trees you can find mosses, ferns, wildflowers, and a variety of shrubs. Only animals prepared for all four seasons can live here, such as the red fox, hawks, woodpeckers, and distinguished cardinals.

TEMPERATE CONIFEROUS FOREST

Take a trip to the coast or into the in-land mountains and you will find the temperate coniferous forests, which enjoy mild winters and heavy rainfall anywhere from 50 to 200 inches per year. Deer, marmot, elk, black bears, and spotted owls are some of the animals that live amongst the dominant and tall evergreen conifers and various deciduous trees.

BOREAL FOREST

Go up north to places like Canada or Scandinavia to find a boreal forest enduring long winters with 15 to 40 inches of precipitation per year (mostly snow, *brrr*) and short summers. The dense canopy is mostly made up of evergreen trees (think spruce, fir, and pine) with only the toughest of animals that have adapted to the extreme cold–deer, moose, elk, caribou, wolves, and grizzly bears, to name a few.

TOP 10 WILDFIRES (BY ACRES)

❶ The Black Friday Bushfire

5 million acres

This widespread destruction occurred in Victoria, Australia on January 13, 1939. The Black Friday Bushfire was one of the most destructive fires the continent had seen and claimed seventy-one lives.

❷ Chinchaga Fire

3.5 million acres

The Chinchaga fire, also known as the Wisp fire, spread throughout northern Alberta and British Columbia in 1950. The most distinguishing feature of this fire was the tremendous billowing smoke it produced.

❸ Miramichi Fire

3 million acres

The Miramichi Fire of October 1825 was one of the deadliest Canada has ever seen. Spread throughout New Brunswick, Canada and parts of Maine, this lethal fire took 160 lives.

❹ Great Fire of 1910, "The Big Burn"

3 million acres

In just two days, the Big Burn of August 1910 demolished 3 million acres of northeastern Washington, northern Idaho, and western Montana. This fire quickly claimed eighty-seven lives.

❺ The Great Michigan Fire

2.5 million acres

On October 8, 1871, Michigan experienced 200 deaths as a result of this widespread fire. In addition to the many lives, 3,000 buildings were destroyed.

❻ Taylor Complex Fire

Up to 1.7 million acres

This disastrous fire occurred on June 12 during the record-breaking 2004 Alaska fire season. The Taylor Complex Fire was a major contributor in the damage Alaska experienced that year.

❼ The Great Fire

1.5 million acres

The Great Fire of 1845 in Oregon was one of several fires the state experienced in the nineteenth century—and one of the largest.

❽ The Peshtigo Fire

1.2 million acres

On the same day as the Great Michigan Fire, Wisconsin experienced terrible wildfires. On October 8, 1871, Wisconsin saw 2,500 deaths—the most deaths by fire in U.S. history.

❾ Cloquet Fire

1.2 million acres

The Cloquet Fire of Minnesota occurred on October 12, 1918. This fire not only burned 1.2 million acres but also claimed 450 lives.

❿ 2008 California Fire Siege

1.2 million acres

California falls victim to wildfires every year, but the summer of 2008 proved especially devastating. During the 2008 California Fire Siege, the sunny state lost thirteen firefighters.

FIELD NOTES

Keep track of everything you discover during your outdoor adventures. Take notes on successful fire-starting methods. Log your cord consumption or seasoning dates. Create packing lists for camping trips. Journal your findings. Sketch the natural world around you. Like John Muir and other naturalists you can record your thoughts and musings as you wander.

ABOUT THE AUTHOR

J. Scott Donahue was a high school freshman in Mr. Hancock's English class when he first read Jon Krakauer's *Into Thin Air*. A decade later, he traveled to Nepal and wrote his Master's thesis composed of essays on travel and conservation. He contributes to *Sierra* magazine and YellowstonePark.com and finds the source of wonder in climbing the high Sierra. He is also the author of *50 Ways to Save the Honey Bees (and Change the World)*.

ABOUT THE ILLUSTRATOR

Gina Baek is a Korean illustrator based in the East Coast of the United States. She studied illustration at Rhode Island School of Design, and her work has been selected by Society of Illustrators LA multiple times. After graduating with her BFA in 2016, Gina started a career as a children's book illustrator. She strives for creating delicate and elaborate images using pencil, watercolor, and pen and ink.

ABOUT CIDER MILL PRESS BOOK PUBLISHERS

Good ideas ripen with time. From seed to harvest,
Cider Mill Press brings fine reading, information,
and entertainment together between the covers of its
creatively crafted books. Our Cider Mill bears fruit twice
a year, publishing a new crop of titles each spring and fall.

"Where Good Books Are Ready for Press"

Visit us on the Web at
www.cidermillpress.com

or write to us at
PO Box 454
12 Spring St.
Kennebunkport, Maine 04046

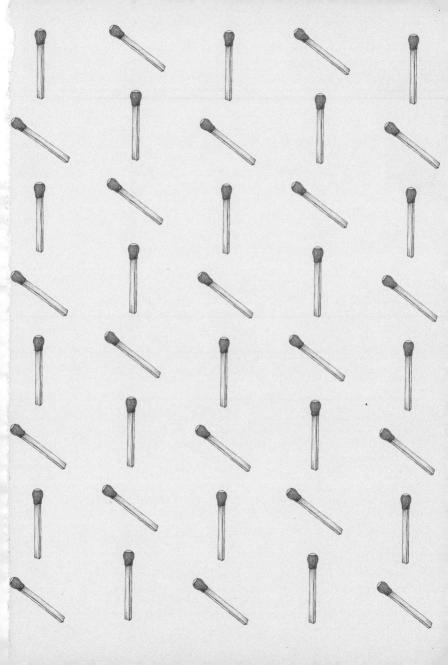

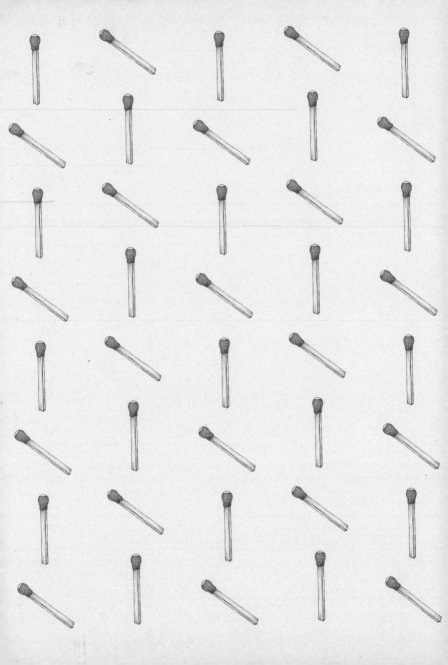